"*Dear teenager, you are not too young* [...]
not too hard, too overwhelming, or [...]
you everything you need for life and g[...]
imagine. That's the message of *Transf[...]*
sage I've personally seen lived out in t[...] of Katherine Forster. Teens, you need to be transformed by truth. It happened to Forster, and in this book, she shares how it can happen to you too. Her writing is accessible, relatable, theological, and highly practical. She'll change how you view the Bible and increase your love for Christ. *Transformed by Truth* is a must-read for the Christian teen."

Jaquelle Crowe Ferris, author, *This Changes Everything: How the Gospel Transforms the Teen Years*

"Convicting, informative, and extremely practical! This book takes you through the *who, what, when, where, why,* and *how* of Bible study in a fun and relatable way. A valuable resource for all Christian teens (and adults)!"

Hannah Leary, Cohost, National Bible Bee

"Christian teens are often embarrassed to admit that they're unsure how to study the Bible—or worse, that they find the Bible boring. With relatable candor and honesty, National Bible Bee champion Katherine Forster goes toe-to-toe with many of the common threats to a teen's biblical literacy. *Transformed by Truth* is filled with solid encouragement and practical tools for teens hoping to develop a joyful dependence on God's word."

Lindsey Carlson, author, *Growing in Godliness: A Teen Girl's Guide to Maturing in Christ*

"This book will inspire you to not only begin memorizing the word of God, but also to pursue a closer relationship with the person of God."

Michael Farris, President and CEO, Alliance Defending Freedom

TRANSFORMED BY TRUTH

KATHERINE FORSTER

Transformed by Truth

WHY AND HOW TO STUDY
THE BIBLE FOR YOURSELF AS A TEEN

CROSSWAY®

WHEATON, ILLINOIS

Cover design: Crystal Courtney

First printing 2019

Printed in the United States of America

Trade paperback ISBN: 978-1-4335-6405-5
ePub ISBN: 978-1-4335-6409-3
PDF ISBN: 978-1-4335-6406-2
Mobipocket ISBN: 978-1-4335-6407-9

Library of Congress Cataloging-in-Publication Data

Names: Forster, Katherine, 1999– author.
Title: Transformed by truth: why and how to study the Bible for yourself as a teen / Katherine Forster.
Description: Wheaton: Crossway, 2019. | Includes bibliographical references.
Identifiers: LCCN 2018041972 (print) | LCCN 2018051811 (ebook) | ISBN 9781433564062 (pdf) | ISBN 9781433564079 (mobi) | ISBN 9781433564093 (epub) | ISBN 9781433564055 (tp)
Subjects: LCSH: Bible—Study and teaching. | Christian teenagers—Religious life.
Classification: LCC BS600.3 (ebook) | LCC BS600.3 .F66 2019 (print) | DDC 220.071–dc23
LC record available at https://lccn.loc.gov/2018041972

Crossway is a publishing ministry of Good News Publishers.

LB		28	27	26	25	24	23	22	21	20	19
15	14	13	12	11	10	9	8	7	6	5	4	3	2	1

To my parents,
for teaching me to seek the Lord
and
to Shelby Kennedy
for her legacy

And we all, with unveiled face,
beholding the glory of the Lord, are being transformed
into the same image from one degree of glory to another.
For this comes from the Lord who is the Spirit.

2 Corinthians 3:18

CONTENTS

ACKNOWLEDGMENTS

Someone occasionally asks me, "So how did you get a book published?" I usually tell them it's a long story. Every step of the way is evidence of God's providence.

Thanks go first to my parents, for making the reading, study, and teaching of the word ubiquitous in our home for as long as I can remember. To my dad, for the long theology conversations; to my mom, for teaching me to love words, editing every chapter of this book, and giving me chocolate.

Thanks to my brothers, Sam and Ben, for putting up with me and encouraging my nerdiness. (*See? I put you in my book.*)

Thank you, Mr. Harre, for telling me to write this book.

Thanks to Jaquelle Crowe, for answering that first clueless email, giving me a place on the editorial team at TheRebelution .com, and most of all for your friendship.

To Brett Harris, for acting as a mentor and guiding me through the world of publishing. Thank you for your advice, your patience, and all the work you put into this project.

To Dave DeWit, for believing in this project, for your kind feedback on my rough drafts, and for being so patient with a new author.

To my amazing team of readers: Carrie-Grace, Sarah, Benji, Isabelle, Nathaniel, and Preston. Your help was invaluable!

To Katya, for your friendship, for patiently listening to me ramble about writing since we were little, and for your constant support.

To Keystone Bible Church, for the teaching, the encouragement, and for being my church family. I love you all.

To all my Bible Bee friends—I wish I had space to name every one of you. I can't tell you how much your friendship means to me.

Finally, to my Lord and Savior Jesus Christ, all thanks and praise. I didn't deserve to write this book, and I didn't have the strength to write this book. But you are faithful to do "far more abundantly than all that we ask or think" (Eph. 3:20). May we always live wholeheartedly for the One who died and rose again on our behalf (2 Cor. 5:14–15).

INTRODUCTION

When I was eight, the Bible was boring.

We read it in church. We read it as a family during evening devotions. My parents even made us read it on our own in the mornings. I was more than passingly familiar with every story. And my eight-year-old self wasn't impressed.

Sure, I might pick up the book of Esther, the same way I would pick up a *Boxcar Children* novel from the library. And I read and reread the more interesting bits of Revelation (like the part about fire-breathing grasshoppers coming out of a bottomless pit). But as to the rest of it? I didn't really care.

When I was thirteen, the Bible was still boring. Now I was reading it, studying it, and even memorizing huge portions for a competition. But it was still just a chore, just something I had to do to be a good Christian, make my parents happy, win prizes, and look good in front of my church friends.

I was missing something. I didn't realize—or didn't fully comprehend—that the Bible was more than just an ancient religious document. It's more than ink on a page, more than a helpful guide to life. It's the very words of the living God.

THE COMPETITION THAT CHANGED ME

In November 2013, I was on a stage in Sevierville, Tennessee. It was the final round of the National Bible Bee Competition. I'd been competing at the local and national level for several years, but I never thought I'd make it that far. I never expected to hear Dr. Michael Farris introduce me as a finalist, and I certainly never expected to win.

The other four finalists and I had memorized hundreds of verses and studied two books of the Bible to be on that stage. We had spent our summer and fall immersed in endless review. And finally, we had arrived. We sat to one side, waiting for our names to be called. "In fifth place . . . In fourth place . . . In third place . . ." Now just one other girl and I were left, grinning nervously at each other. "In second place . . ."

When my name wasn't called for second place, I knew. I had won first place in my division!

Winning was a huge surprise—I knew it was by God's grace alone. But something much bigger had also happened that year. Up until then, I had studied and memorized the Bible, but I was bothered by how little I loved God. I could rattle off his words, but they were just words to me. My Christian life seemed shallow, apathetic, and lacking.

That year, something changed. I had accumulated so much knowledge about God, but now it became personal. The words weren't just words anymore. God used his truth in my heart to give me a greater love for him. Before I ever stepped onto that stage, I had begun to discover that the real prize was so much bigger than a crystal trophy—it was the joy of knowing and walking with God as I met him through his word.

THE CHALLENGE WE NEED

The Bible Bee taught me to dig deeply into God's word for myself. I learned how to search out the meaning of a passage and connect it to other parts of Scripture. I encountered glorious truths about God and the gospel, and biblical principles started to inform my thinking. My relationship with God grew in ways I could never have dreamed.

Learning how to study God's word for myself changed my life.

But I also realized something that saddened me: *few teenagers are being challenged to study and memorize God's word seriously.* Often, the highest challenge we're given is to read the Bible regularly. And even that's not always the case—it's considered normal for us to leave our Bible on the shelf for weeks on end, never even picking it up.

This can't be the best there is for us! We desperately need God's words because we need God. Our Creator and Savior has spoken to us. This is how we can know him: through what he himself has said.

Shouldn't we be pursuing the knowledge of our Maker with all that we are? We need more than a nice-looking book that sits on a shelf. We need more than a few minutes of devotional reading every morning. We need to take the time, energy, and commitment to dive into God's word and search out the truth he has given us.

THIS BOOK IS FOR YOU

Maybe the Bible is boring to you too. Or maybe you love God's word and want to dive deeper into it but don't know where to start. Maybe you aren't familiar with the Bible, and you don't see what the fuss is about.

Wherever you are, this book is for you. It's meant to encourage you to go deeper in your knowledge of God through his word— to do something this world would say is too hard or too boring for teenagers. And it's meant to equip you—to give you the tools you need to study the Bible for yourself.

This book has two parts. The first five chapters talk about the *why* of Bible study: why it's important for teens, how God has revealed himself to us through his word, the great story it tells, how it tells us about God's will for our lives, and how it helps us to obey him.

Chapters 6 through 11 talk about the *how* of Bible study. We'll talk about very practical things such as what inductive Bible study

Introduction

is, how to make it a habit, how to actually go about studying a book of the Bible, and what application really looks like.

My hope is that you'll come away from this book with a renewed vision of why Bible study is important and with the tools to pursue it on your own. Teens need serious Bible study just as much as adults. That's why this book was written: to challenge you to a higher view of God's word and a greater commitment to your walk with Christ.

A SIGNPOST, NOT A DESTINATION

Whenever my family goes on a road trip, I like to watch the signs along the interstate: "45 more miles to Orlando" or "102 miles to Atlanta." The signs tell us which direction we're going and how far away our destination is. But they're not destinations themselves. We don't really care that much about the sign—we care about the city or location to which it's directing us.

This book is like one of those signs. It's not a destination in itself. You don't need my wisdom or experience. You need God's word. This book is a signpost pointing you to that awesome truth.

My prayer is that as you read this book—and long after you finish—you'll develop the skill and habit of studying God's word. I pray that you'll grow in your knowledge of him and that your relationship with your Savior will be strengthened. I pray that the truth you absorb will penetrate every fiber of your being and transform you into the image of Christ.

PART 1

WHY?

1

YOU ARE NOT TOO YOUNG

When I was little, there was a song we sang all the time in Sunday school:

> *Read your Bible,*
> *pray every day—pray every day—pray every day.*
> *Read your Bible,*
> *pray every day,*
> *and you'll grow—grow—grow!*

Reading the Bible is essential to our spiritual growth. Every good teacher or pastor will tell you to read your Bible regularly. Read a chapter a day, or several verses, or use a reading plan. The Bible is a book—it's God's own communication to us.

It's meant to be read.

If we're not setting aside time to read it, there's a serious problem.

However, *reading* the Bible is only the beginning.

We have to start there, but we can't stop there. The Bible is brimming with truth that requires deep, diligent study to discover. Deeper study reveals realities about God, insights into human nature, commands, instructions, and beautiful promises that we might never have seen or understood otherwise.

Simply reading the Bible is like visiting the Smoky Mountains of Tennessee in autumn and never getting out of the car. You'll get a spectacular view. You'll enjoy the beauty of mountain ranges with their blanket of gold and crimson trees. You might even get to see rural homes and businesses with their quirky, whimsical autumn yard decorations.

But you won't enjoy hot, fried apple pies in a farm store. You won't hike up a mountain, take a picture in front of a waterfall, and get soaked trying to jump between rocks as you make your way back down a creek.

I love the Smoky Mountains, and I have great memories of driving through the towns and surrounding countryside with my family. But all my best memories are the ones where we got out of the car and went on an adventure.

In that sense, the Bible is a little bit like the mountains. You can stay where it's comfortable, content to read a little bit every day. And you will gain from the experience—make no mistake! The Holy Spirit will always work through his word to teach you more about God and make you more like him.

But you can also go deeper. You can devote the time and effort to searching for truths that lend themselves to vigorous, diligent study. You can learn more about our God and stand in awe as you see his glory more clearly in his word.

You can get out of your comfort zone and go on an adventure.

INEXHAUSTIBLE RICHES

For several years, probably the oldest person in our church was Dr. Spotts. He was a tall, kind, white-haired old man, and we joked that he was a walking Bible encyclopedia. If we had a question about the Bible, we would ask him, and he could always answer. He probably knew more about the Bible than all of us combined!

A few years ago, just after Dr. Spotts's death, our pastor said something that has stuck with me ever since. He had asked Dr. Spotts why he kept studying the Bible, even though he seemed to know everything about it. Dr. Spotts had answered, "There's still so much I don't know!"

When you grow up in Sunday school and know all the stories—from David and Goliath to the gory tales in Judges and all the acts of the apostles—it's very tempting to think you know everything there is to know about the Bible. In fact, I used to think that if I studied and memorized too much, I would get to a point where there was nothing left to learn. I actually thought I could somehow "arrive," and the rest of my Christian life would be boring because I would already know it all! But as I started studying in more depth, I quickly realized my mistake. There's more in the Bible than entire lifetimes of study put together could begin to comprehend.

The psalmist said, "My mouth will tell of your righteous acts, of your deeds of salvation all the day, for *their number is past my knowledge*" (Ps. 71:15). God is infinite—there's no end to him or to what we can learn about him. If we could ever fully understand him, he wouldn't be God.

We think we know so much—but what if that's just because we've only scratched the surface?

The Bible is like a gold mine: it's full of rich truth to comfort, convict, and bring us joy in God, and we can never exhaust those riches. The more we learn, the more there will be to learn. The deeper we dig, the more we'll see what unexplored depths lie beneath.

We can't be content to live on the surface when so many riches lie below. Yes, there are treasures up here, plain to see. But why would we stay here if we have the opportunity for so much more? Yes, it takes work. You're going to encounter difficulties along with outright opposition from the devil, the world around you, and the sin inside yourself. But what you'll discover is worth it.

21

OUR PURPOSE: TO KNOW GOD

Chances are, you haven't been challenged to intensive Bible study before. You might think this is only for leaders and teachers—your pastors, seminary professors, and the authors who write books for other Christians to read.

But Bible study is not just an academic pursuit, and it's not something that's only important for certain Christians. It's the pursuit of something that's fundamental to all our lives: the knowledge of God.

God gave us the Bible so we could know him—not just know about him, but have a relationship with him. Jesus Christ himself came so that we could know God (1 John 5:20). This is our purpose and our greatest joy.

As J. I. Packer wrote, "What were we made for? To know God. What aim should we set ourselves in life? To know God. What is the 'eternal life' that Jesus gives? Knowledge of God. . . . What is the best thing in life, bringing more joy, delight, and contentment, than anything else? Knowledge of God."[1] The Bible isn't just another piece of literature. Neither is it a magic book. It's God's words to us about himself. It's the way he has given us to know him.

And it isn't just for adults. "How can a *young man* keep his way pure? By guarding it according to your word" (Ps. 119:9). The Bible is for you. It's for me. It's for teens and little children as well as for adults. God has spoken to us—young men and women—just as surely as he has spoken to our parents and grandparents and pastors and little siblings.

If he has spoken to us, shouldn't we listen? If our Creator has told us about himself, shouldn't we learn everything we can about what he's said?

Thus says the LORD: "Let not a wise man boast in his wisdom, and let not the mighty man boast in his might, let not a rich man boast in his riches, but let him who boasts boast in this, that he understands and knows me, that I am the LORD who practices steadfast love, justice, and righteousness on earth. For in these things I delight," declares the LORD. (Jer. 9:23–24)

We have the awesome gift of the knowledge of God—and the awesome responsibility to pursue that knowledge in his word. That's what inductive Bible study (what we'll be discussing in this book) is about. It isn't some mysterious practice reserved for seminarians. It's the discipline and method of knowing and understanding what God has said to us. And it's for you and me.

WE'RE NOT TOO YOUNG

This kind of serious study is antithetical to our society's expectations for teens. On one hand, pop culture defines "teenagerhood" as a sacred space for having fun and letting important, serious things wait until later. The music industry praises the culture of drinking, getting high, and forgetting about consequences. Movies consistently depict teens as shallow, rebellious, and obsessed with romance (while also somehow wiser than the adults around them).

On the other hand, the teen years are often defined by achievement. They're presented as the opportunity to accomplish and pursue everything from good grades to sports trophies. While achievement is a good thing, we often make it an idol. It's easy to spend all our time and energy chasing grades, scholarships, awards, money, or success.

This is what the world tells us: that because we're young, we don't have the time, ability, or need for something as serious, rigorous, and demanding as personal Bible study. It tells us that sort of thing isn't important until we're older. It tells us either that now is the time to have fun and not worry about that stuff, or that now is the time to chase every other kind of achievement.

What the world doesn't tell you is that "right now" is exactly when Bible study is important. We can't wait until we're older. These teen years are formative. They're the foundation for who we're going to be for the rest of our lives. We have a choice. We can waste these years—or we can use them for God's glory, drawing closer to him and preparing for what lies ahead.

What the world doesn't tell you is that if you spend all your teen years merely chasing fun or achievement, you'll come up empty. You'll dive into the waves, looking for the treasure you're certain is there. You'll grab it and hold on tight, but, when you surface, all you'll find is a handful of broken shells.

Having fun and seeking success aren't wrong; these things are good gifts from God. But if that's all we pursue during this season, we'll find we're chasing emptiness, and we'll enter adulthood seriously ill-equipped to handle the challenges life will throw at us. We must aim higher.

And here's the thing: we already work hard. We work hard to do well in school, get that college acceptance letter, be an entrepreneur, make that goal, or to get to the next level on that video game. So why do we think we shouldn't have to work hard at what is more important than any of those things—our relationship with the God who created us?

Author and teacher Jen Wilkin writes,

> Students understand that what is important is worth our time and effort to attain. They regularly invest long hours, not just in their schoolwork, but in their sports team, music lessons, dance classes, or jobs. . . . What if we asked them to learn to rightly divide the Word with all the discipline they would apply to learning calculus or the violin or gymnastics?[2]

What if we asked that of ourselves?

We're so used to thinking about the Bible as just an addition to our already-busy lives of study and work. But it should be the center of our lives, the most important subject we study. We need to be willing to set aside time and mental energy for it. Our relationship with God should take priority—and when it does, everything else will fall into its proper place.

BUT WHAT IF I MESS UP?

For a long time, I was scared to study the Bible on my own. I was only a teenager. I didn't have seminary training like my pastor. I didn't have many years of experience like my parents. What if I got something wrong?

Maybe you feel that way too. Maybe you're afraid of messing something up or not understanding. Here's the thing, though: God didn't set age limits on the Bible. He didn't write Philippians for high schoolers and Genesis for elementary kids, Ephesians for adults and Deuteronomy for seminary professors. His revelation is for teens too. All of the Bible is for all of us.

Yes, some parts of the Bible are harder to understand (we've all scratched our heads reading Revelation). But the Bible isn't something you can only comprehend once you've taken seminary classes or once you turn thirty. There aren't hidden meanings you can only understand once you've been initiated into a special club.

Learning more about the Bible through classes or special training certainly helps. I'm very glad my pastors have been to seminary! Experience and maturity are important too. We need to value all these things in our parents and older Christians. But you don't have to wait to have them before you can start to understand the Bible for yourself.

This isn't because we're naturally so smart or spiritual—as humans, we're weak and inadequate. We'll meet great opposition and difficulty along the way. If we had to do this on our own, we would be right to be scared!

But we aren't on our own in our quest to understand God's word. He hasn't left us to try and figure it out by ourselves. He *wants* us to know him. That should give us great confidence!

He has promised us help. James 1:5 says that if we need wisdom, we should just ask—and if we ask in faith, God will answer and give it to us. Wisdom is essential to Bible study, and God has promised it freely!

He has also given us the Holy Spirit. This is an amazing gift—God himself lives inside us! The Holy Spirit—the author of Scripture—works in our hearts to help us understand and apply his word.

He has also given us help from other people. Older and more experienced Christians often have insight that can help us understand what we're studying. If you're blessed with godly parents, go to them first with questions. You also probably have access to pastors or mature men and women in your church who can answer questions and help you think through difficult truths.

Often we can find assistance in commentaries and sermons as well. A good commentary or sermon is the result of intense Bible study and a great depth of knowledge of the Bible, and they can be wonderful tools. (We'll discuss commentaries and other tools more in chapter 10.)

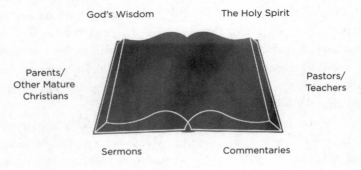

God's Wisdom   The Holy Spirit

Parents/ Other Mature Christians

Pastors/ Teachers

Sermons   Commentaries

Illustration 1.1: Study Helps

EXPERIENCE IT YOURSELF

This brings up a point you may already be wondering. Why do we even need to study the Bible for ourselves? If there are so many books and sermons and commentaries, can't we just use those? These books were written by people who really know what they're talking about. Won't you learn more from them than you will on your own? Well, let me share an illustration.

Imagine you're at a party, which is taking place at a house on the beach. It's evening, the sun is going down—and it's freezing cold. A few of your friends decide to go down to the water's edge and watch the last of the sunset. Now you have a choice: you can either stay inside the warm house and eat cookies, or you can go out in the cold and watch the sun sink into the ocean in a blaze of color.

If you stay inside you'll be warm, and your friends could probably tell you about it—they could tell you how beautiful it was, about the seagulls crying in the air, and how boats were silhouetted against the sun. They could even show you pictures! But if you go outside and brave the cold, you can experience it for yourself in a way no picture or description could ever match.

Bible study is a little bit like that. We can have other people tell us about the Bible—and we'll learn a lot. I'm not trying to discount books or commentaries at all. These have great value in our spiritual lives. And I'm certainly not suggesting you stop listening to your pastor's sermons! However, if you *only* ever listen to what other people tell you, you'll never experience it on your own.

Studying the Bible allows you to discover the truth for yourself. It's the active process of exploring, rather than the passive process of listening. And as you labor to search out and understand it, you'll find you own that truth. It will become a part of you.

Someone else can tell you how great God's love is—but it will probably impact you a lot more when you study 1 John 4 and learn about how God sent his only begotten Son to give us life.

You'll stand in awe as you dig into the meaning of words like "propitiation," meditate on Christ's sacrifice, and ponder how it displays true love.

Discovering these things for yourself is more difficult, but it brings so much joy.

IT WILL BE HARD

I'm not going to try to convince you to study your Bible by telling you it doesn't take too much work, or it doesn't take a lot of time. It does. It does take time, and it does take effort.

The question, then, becomes, "Is it worth it?" That's the question you have to answer for yourself, in your own life. Is studying the Bible—is knowing your Savior—as important as school? As sports or your social media feed or Netflix or a hobby? Can you make Bible study a priority? Of course we'll say it's important, but do we live out that belief from day to day in our choices about how we use our time and energy?

You won't always feel like studying the Bible. It won't always feel enjoyable, and sometimes you'll struggle to prioritize it. But is it important enough to push through boredom, early-morning grogginess, or the temptation to do something more fun?

You will probably be frustrated as you're learning. It may feel alien, unnatural, to study the Bible with methods like what you might use in literature class. Bible study is a skill, and just like any other skill, it takes time to learn.

In addition, the world, the devil, and your own sinful flesh all want to keep you from studying the Bible. You will face opposition, whether it's doubt, fear, busyness, or even the temptation of pride at what you're learning.

It's going to be hard. And if we try to do this on our own, we're going to fail. Only God's strength is sufficient. We are inadequate, but his power is perfected in our weakness (2 Cor. 12:9). We'll need to come to him again and again, confessing our sin and weakness and pleading for his strength to overcome every opposition to our study of his word.

This may be the hardest—and the most important—thing you ever do. Persevere, my friend, in his strength! You will find it is more than worth it.

QUESTIONS

1. What problems do you see with our culture's expectations for teenagers? What are you doing to combat those expectations?

2. How are you currently engaging with God's word? What do you want to change or do differently?

3. Why is studying the Bible for yourself important? Is there anything that makes you reluctant to begin?

2

HOW GOD REVEALS HIMSELF

When I was in high school, I had to read *The Iliad* and *The Odyssey*.

These ancient, epic poems were written in a language very similar to that of the New Testament, several hundred years before the birth of Christ. They're gory and, to us, sometimes boring. But the fascinating thing is that they lay out the belief system of an entire culture. The people of ancient Greece actually believed in the reality of Zeus, Achilles, Athena, and Odysseus.

That might lead us to wonder: How is the Bible different from *The Iliad* and *The Odyssey*? For that matter, how is it different from any other ancient piece of religious literature that's been handed down for the past few millennia?

And then, why is the Bible *still* a bestselling book, after so long? Why do so many people—not just scholars and bored high school students—read it every day? Why have ordinary men and women, kings and queens, pastors, monks, and scholars over the centuries given their time, money, and even lives to have this book and to get it into the hands of others?

What's so special about the Bible? Why is it so important? It's essential we answer this question before we go further. If the

Bible is just another ancient document, the book you're reading is a waste of time. Why would I devote so much time and effort to writing a book about Bible study? Why would you read it? Why would you use your time and energy to put these principles into practice?

How is the Bible different from any other book?

If the Bible is merely one more book written by men, then all of *this* is a waste of time. You had better go read a textbook or a novel. However, if the Bible is what it claims to be—the very words of God himself—then it holds the answers to our biggest questions and deserves all of our attention.

IS ANYONE OUT THERE?

The most central and important question anyone can ask is, "Is there a God?" And along with that, "What is this God like?"

This is a vital issue. It might seem like a philosophical query that's irrelevant to our daily lives, but it's more relevant than anything else. It's the question of who created us, why we're here, who defines right and wrong, what is our ultimate destiny, and what gives meaning to our lives.

Today, for example, we're seeing what happens when a culture decides God doesn't exist. Our culture looks at God as a myth, a product of wishful thinking, or at best, as some higher being that maybe does exist but doesn't really care about life on earth.

The problem is, if God isn't really there—or if he is there, but he's silent and uninterested—then who makes the rules? Who decides what's right and wrong? Humans? Does everybody get to decide for themselves? What if right and wrong don't exist at all?

If God doesn't exist as the ultimate standard of good and evil, then you can't say it's right to help people in need. You can't say it's wrong to cheat someone out of money. You can't call it evil when someone kills a child or rampages through a building with a gun.

When a society chooses to believe that God is either not there or is silent and removed, then confusion, chaos, and corruption will reign.

CREATION'S TESTIMONY

But God is there. The simplest look at the world around us reveals it would be foolishness to think otherwise.

The Reformer and author John Calvin wrote, "On each of his works his glory is engraven in characters so bright, so distinct, and so illustrious, that none, however dull and illiterate, can plead ignorance as their excuse."[1] The universe doesn't just whisper about God—it shouts from every corner.

From the order and majesty—even the very existence—of creation, we can infer that there must be a Creator. And from the existence of things such as logic and morals (not to mention the beauty we see every day and the gifts of taste and smell), we have to conclude that this is a good God.

Romans 1:20 says, "For his invisible attributes, namely, his eternal power and divine nature, have been clearly perceived, ever since the creation of the world in the things that have been made. So they are without excuse." God's creation declares his glory, shows us that he exists, and can even tell us something about him. The beauty and evidence of design in the world around us, as well as the knowledge of good and evil imprinted on our own souls, are unmistakable evidence of a good and wise Creator.

However, that's not enough. John Calvin wrote, "In vain for us, therefore, does Creation exhibit so many bright lamps lighted up to show forth the glory of its Author. Though they beam upon us from every quarter, they are altogether insufficient of themselves to lead us into the right path."[2] Even though God has made himself known to some extent through his creation, our hearts are blind. We see the majesty of creation, and we may even deduce something about God from it, but that will never lead us to a true knowledge of him. It will never awaken true worship in us.

Calvin continues, "We are deficient in natural powers which might enable us to rise to a pure and clear knowledge of God."[3] Unless God opens our eyes and awakens faith in our hearts, we'll never see his glory and praise him as we should.

Not only that, but even if our eyes were opened to see the majesty of God in his creation, that still wouldn't be enough. Think about it—even if we saw and understood everything about God that we possibly could from his creation, what would we know? We might perceive that he is good, infinite, eternal, and many other things. And we would know that we don't measure up to the standard of perfection he sets.

That would leave us hopeless—knowing that we've offended a holy God and rightfully deserve to be punished but not knowing anything we could do about it.

HE IS THERE, AND HE IS NOT SILENT

If we knew that God was there but didn't know anything else about him, we would only have cause for despair. We would still have no answers to our basic questions—*Who am I? Why am I here? Why is there so much evil, pain, and suffering in this world?*

The American philosopher and theologian Francis Schaeffer wrote an entire trilogy of books dealing with these questions. He writes, "The infinite-personal God is there, but also *He is not silent*; that changes the whole world."[4]

This piercing, glorious truth is the answer not only to our society's confusion, but our own. God is there. God has spoken. God has told us who he is and who we are; he has defined right and wrong; and most importantly, he has told us how we can be saved from the just punishment of our sin and have restored fellowship with him.

How has he done this? In Scripture. Schaeffer writes, "Beginning with the Christian system as God has given it to men in . . . the Bible one can move along and find that every area of life is touched by truth and a song."[5] The fact that God has spoken impacts every single aspect of our lives.

We asked why anyone would put their time, energy, and resources into studying the Bible. This is why. God's word to us is the answer to our cultural chaos. More importantly, it's the answer to the problem each of us has: *How can I know God?*

WHAT IS THE BIBLE?

Now we can see how the Bible is different from *The Iliad* and *The Odyssey* and every other book ever written. Those books were written by men. They were a human's attempt to imagine what God might be like. They tried to create God in man's image—to "measure him by their own carnal stupidity," as Calvin puts it.[6]

But the Bible is different. Instead of us trying to figure out God, the Bible is God telling us about himself.

It may sound odd to say that "God revealed himself" through what's essentially a collection of documents written by various men in ancient times. While some portions of the Bible were specifically dictated by God himself, most of it was written by humans using their own words.

However, those words were not merely their own. In numerous places throughout the Bible, we find the claim that these are the words of God. Sometimes God spoke directly to individuals, who then wrote down what he said (Jer. 1:1–2; Ezek. 1:3; 2 Pet. 1:20–21). More often the authors wrote in their own name, but God was the one inspiring the very words they wrote (2 Tim. 3:16). Author and long-time pastor John Piper explains it this way: "The Holy Spirit worked in and through the human authors so that the words were really their own way of writing, but expressed God's meaning with the words he willed for them to use."[7]

Most of the biblical authors were not just scribes writing down the words God dictated to them. When you read these writings—especially the New Testament—you can see their unique personalities and styles. Luke writes in refined, educated Greek. Some of the former fishermen use rather bad Greek and employ the Hebrew expressions with which they would have been more familiar. Paul uses extremely long and complicated sentences, and as an educated man, is skilled at addressing both Greeks and Jews with terms and analogies familiar to their cultural contexts.

Nevertheless, the Holy Spirit was actively working in and through their writing so that their very words were inspired by God. "For no prophecy was ever produced by the will of man, but *men spoke from God as they were carried along by the Holy Spirit*" (2 Pet. 1:21). In 2 Timothy 3:16, Paul writes that "*all* Scripture is breathed out by God." He was speaking of the Old Testament scriptures here, but in other places he himself specifically claims to be inspired by the Holy Spirit (1 Cor. 7:40). In 2 Peter 3:15–16, Peter calls Paul's writings Scripture, putting them on the same level as the Old Testament.

The Bible is both divinely inspired and written in human words. This is a marvelous grace of God! He has shown us himself yet in human language and words we understand. Because of that, we can read, study, and communicate this truth about him to others. Praise God!

THE BIBLE'S BOOKS

The books of the Bible are separate and distinct, each written by its own author and for a particular audience. Yet, together, they make up the overarching story of the Bible—and their consistency is evidence of God's hand in their writing.

The Bible is divided into what we call the Old and New Testaments. The Old Testament is also known as the Hebrew scriptures, or *Tanak*, and it would have been the only "Bible" that

Jesus and his disciples used. While the Hebrew scriptures arrange the books differently, they contain the same content as the Old Testament that's in our Bibles today.

The Old Testament is the record of God's dealings with mankind from creation until four hundred years before Christ. It records the fall of mankind, the promise of the coming Savior, and the history of the nation of Israel, God's chosen people. It contains thirty-nine books.

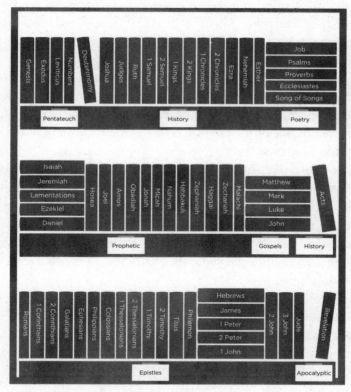

Illustration 2.1: The Books of the Bible

The Hebrew scriptures were the only "Bible" available to the first Christians. They were the only writings at the time that had been inspired by God. But when Jesus came into the world as God incarnate, he gave the authority for a second collection of writings. John Piper explains that "the person and the teaching of Jesus must inevitably lead to an expansion of the canon of the early church."[8] This led to what we call the New Testament—a collection of God-inspired writings with authority to guide and govern believers.

This was accomplished primarily through the apostles. Jesus chose twelve men to be his followers—those he would send out to be the foundation of his church as they proclaimed the gospel. He promised to send the Holy Spirit, who would guide them into all truth (John 16:13).

The books of the New Testament, which we call *apostolic*, were not all written by those twelve men. Luke, for instance, was not an apostle. Paul was made an apostle by Christ, even though he was not one of the original twelve. James and Jude were not apostles, although they were physically half-brothers of Jesus. Piper explains, "Apostolicity is the supernatural transmission of naturally incomprehensible reality to spiritually discerning people ('those who are spiritual,' 1 Cor. 2:13), through writing that is 'taught by the Spirit.'"[9] The men who wrote the New Testament were either apostles or closely associated with them, but the true authority behind their writings is the inspiration of the Holy Spirit.

The New Testament contains twenty-seven books. Four of these are Gospels, twenty-two are epistles, and one is apocalyptic (see Illustration 2.1).

GOD'S REVELATION OF HIMSELF

Every book of the Bible reveals God, but each does it in beautifully diverse ways.

In the Old Testament books that deal with the history of Israel, we see that God is the all-powerful, preexisting Creator.

We see the way he deals with mankind—through covenants. We see his faithfulness to his promises and his covenant people. We see his sovereignty over history, and we see his character expressed through the law.

In books like Isaiah and Jeremiah, where God spoke to his people Israel through men he appointed as prophets, he displays his justice and holiness. He demonstrates his righteousness by not leaving evil unpunished. He also demonstrates his great compassion and declares the hope of redemption—both in Christ's first coming and ultimately in the restoration of this world.

In the biblical books of poetry, God's character is revealed in myriad ways. The Psalms are full of truths about him. We see, for instance, that he invites us to cry out to him in our troubles, but also that he is the grounds of complete confidence and trust. In Proverbs, we learn that he's a God of wisdom. Ecclesiastes shows the pointlessness of life without him. In the Song of Solomon (or Song of Songs), we see that he is the author of love.

The Gospels are the story of Jesus, and in these narratives we see our Lord in all his glory—the paradoxical glory of the majestic Creator God humbling himself infinitely in order to save his creation. The Gospels show us both the humanity and deity of Jesus Christ as they narrate the essential aspects of his righteous life, his death, and his resurrection.

Acts continues where the Gospels leave off, telling the story of the early church after Christ's ascension into heaven. From this book, we get most of our knowledge about the first-century church, and especially of how Jews and non-Jews were united for the first time in Christ. Again, we see God's sovereignty as he orchestrated events in the first century.

The epistles—letters from church fathers to different churches and individuals—explain and apply the gospel. They were written by apostles (especially by Paul) and other men who had a close association with Jesus. They lay out theology for the church and explain how we should live now that God has saved us.

Revelation is the one apocalyptic book of the Bible. Written by the apostle John, it relates his visions of the end times. Although it may be the hardest book of the Bible to understand, it's important because it shows us the end of the story with startling detail. God is not done with this world—he has a plan, and he will bring it to completion!

HOW IT GOT HERE

Imagine you want to read the Bible, but you don't have a copy. You walk into your local Christian bookstore and ask the cashier where to find the Bibles. She directs you to the correct section of the store—and you discover a jumble of scrolls covered with ancient Greek letters.

Of course, that would be absurd! Our Bibles today look like regular books, and most of the time they come in whatever language we grew up speaking. Your Bible may even be an app or a website.

But Moses, David, and Paul didn't write English or Spanish; they wrote ancient Hebrew and Greek. They didn't type on computers either; they probably wrote with a quill on parchment or papyrus scrolls.

So how did these ancient writings get to us?

Once all the books had been written, they were compiled into the Old and New Testament *canons*. The canons are simply the collections of books that ancient Israel, and then the early church, recognized were inspired by God. Paul Wegner explains, "The [Old Testament] books did not receive their authority because they were placed into the canon; rather, they were recognized by the nation of Israel as having divine authority, and were therefore included in the canon."[10] The same holds true for the books of the New Testament. The Jewish leaders and church fathers who compiled these books into a single collection didn't give the books their authority—they recognized the authority these books possessed because of their divine inspiration. Today, we recognize the Old and New Testament books together as a single canon: the entirety of God's word to us.

These books were reproduced by copyists over hundreds of years (remember, this was before computers and "copy-paste"!). God used both professional scribes and ordinary people to preserve his written word for centuries. The number and age of the copies we have confirms that this preservation was little short of miraculous.

However, this was all in the original languages. Most of us don't know ancient Hebrew and Greek! No matter how well the books were preserved, we can't read them today unless we take years of language classes. That's where translators come in.

Translators are scholars who have great skill in the languages that were used to write the Bible originally. They make sure the meaning of the words in the Bible we read (whether English, Spanish, or any other language) is as close as possible to the meaning of the words in the original text. These men and women are an invaluable gift to God's church.

If you've ever wondered why we have so many "Bible versions," this is why! Each group of translators will use slightly different words and grammar in their translation, even though the text they're translating from is the same. Older translations like the King James Version will also differ from newer ones like the English Standard Version because our own language changes.

The many translations we have today can be confusing, especially when you're trying to buy a Bible. There are many good ones out there, but it's important to realize that some translations are of a higher quality than others. Specifically, you should look for a translation that translates the actual Greek and Hebrew words as closely as possible (the pages in the front often contain some notes on the translators' philosophy).

By God's grace, we have many excellent translations today! A few good English ones are the English Standard Version (ESV), the New American Standard Bible (NASB), and the King James Version (KJV). Some of these can sound very different—for instance, the KJV was translated in the early seventeenth century, so its language is often archaic (although beautiful). The NASB and ESV, on the other hand, use more modern language.

HOW DO WE KNOW IT'S TRUE?

This book is written with the assumption that the Bible is in fact what it claims to be—that is, the true and divinely inspired word of God. If it's not, Bible study would be pointless or even dangerous. But if the Bible is God's word, then studying and knowing it is one of the most important things we could ever do because it allows us to know God himself.

This assumption is not a groundless one. I don't just believe in the Bible because it's what I've always known—or because it's practical to do so—and neither should you. We should believe what we do because it is really true.

That's why it's okay to ask questions like, "How can I know the Bible is really the word of God?" Our faith isn't baseless—there are good and convincing reasons to believe the Bible. Asking questions won't destroy your faith; in fact, looking for answers can actually strengthen your faith, because the answers are there to find. Christianity isn't a religious system that collapses if you think about it too hard. The truth can stand up to the toughest questions.

If you're already a believer, it's likely there will come a time when you'll have to wrestle with why you believe what you believe. If you've never understood why it makes sense to believe the Bible, my prayer is that you will.

There are many good reasons to believe the Bible is true. Unfortunately, there isn't room here to go into them all or to give extended explanations. However, perhaps the most convincing argument is the Bible itself.

John Calvin writes that "Scripture bears upon the face of it as clear evidence of its truth, as white and black do of their color, sweet and bitter their taste."[11] If this is true, we don't need to read a lot of long, complex books before we can know for ourselves that the Bible is really God's word. We can see it for ourselves as we read and study. *The Westminster Catechism*, a document from the seventeenth century laying out Christian beliefs, argues, "The scriptures manifest themselves to be the word of God, by . . . the scope of the whole, which is to give all glory to God."[12]

This is the point of John Piper's excellent book, *A Peculiar Glory*, which I've been quoting throughout this chapter. God's glory is manifest in the Scriptures, revealing itself in every command, every narrative, and the way they all fit together in the broad story of redemption. "This pervasive aim of the Scriptures to glorify God, in what they teach and how they teach it, reveals the handiwork of God in the writing of the Bible."[13] The way Scripture glorifies God is the best evidence for its truth.

This glory is everywhere in Scripture, but we won't see it until God opens our eyes to see "the light of the knowledge of the glory of God in the face of Jesus Christ" (2 Cor. 4:6). Our eyes are blinded to his beauty and perfection; his Spirit has to do a work in our hearts before we can see it. But as our eyes are opened, we behold God in the meaning of these words and see a kind of glory that's displayed by no other book, no other doctrine in this world.

Countless books have been written about the Bible's truthfulness. Scholars and pastors much more learned than we are have dealt with subjects such as supposed contradictions in the Bible, historical proofs, the resurrection, and difficult topics such as how evil can exist. Books like this can be very helpful in strengthening our own faith and explaining it to others. If you'd like to read more on this subject, Appendix A contains several resources.

For now, however, we'll turn from talking about what the Bible *is* to what it *says*—the great and true story it tells. That will be the subject of the next chapter.

QUESTIONS

1. Why is it so important that God has spoken to us directly? How does that affect you personally?

2. Do you think society today has rejected the fact that God exists and has spoken? Where do you see the consequences of this rejection?

3. Have you ever struggled with doubting the truth of God's word? What helped you believe? Or, if you're not sure if you believe, what questions are you struggling with?

3

THE BIG STORY

The Bible has been called a lot of things: "God's love letter to us," "an ancient religious document," "a handbook for living," or "Basic Instructions Before Leaving Earth."

All those things are true—it is an ancient religious document, it does tell of God's love for us, and it contains instructions for living. But none of those names tell the whole story either.

Because that's what the Bible is—the whole story.

IT'S CALLED *METANARRATIVE*

Often, we think of the Bible in terms of snippets and bits and pieces. We see it as disconnected parts rather than a whole. There's a story here and a bit of wisdom there; David and Goliath show us the value of trusting God, and Matthew 5:13–16 tells us to be the light of the world.

But there's more to it than that.

As we talked about in the last chapter, even though the books of the Bible were written by more than forty different authors at different times throughout history, God was inspiring them all. God—the all-powerful, personal Creator of this world—had planned out how he would communicate himself to mankind from before the foundation of the earth.

Because God was behind all these writings, inspiring the authors and sovereign over the events they recorded, the Bible tells one cohesive, true story.

All the other stories, instructions, and promises fall into the framework of this one, overarching story. Genesis, 1 Samuel, Ezekiel, Mark, 2 Thessalonians, Revelation—they're all like scenes in a play. Each of them advances the plot or forms a subplot to enhance the main narrative.

This main narrative is called a *metanarrative*: one story that acts as the umbrella over all the other stories. You can see small examples of metanarrative in novels and movies today. It might be a series of books, a show, or a movie franchise. Each book, episode, or movie tells its own story (and hopefully has a satisfying conclusion), but they all fit into the larger story that the series or show or movie franchise is telling. (The Star Wars movies and the Marvel cinematic universe are some of the best-known examples of these metanarratives today.)

The Bible is the greatest metanarrative of all time, because it takes all time under its umbrella. It tells the story of history, beginning with creation and ending with the new creation.

It's time we stop thinking of the Bible as a collection of disjointed, unconnected stories and instructions, and start thinking of it as the cohesive, consistent, true story it really is.

THE SOURCE OF ALL THE STORIES

Are you familiar with these terms: *protagonist, antagonist, setting, inciting incident, rising action, climax,* and *resolution*? These are standard elements of pretty much every story ever told—whether it's *The Odyssey* or *Wonder Woman*.

We start with the *setting*, where everything is okay (or at least normal) for the *protagonist* (our main character). But then the *antagonist* (the bad guy or thing) comes along and ruins it. This is the *inciting incident*, and it sets off a train of events where the main character/protagonist is trying to get everything back to a good state or *resolution*.

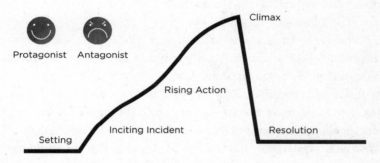

Illustration 3.1: Elements of a Story

The bulk of the story consists of this *rising action*, where the main character/protagonist makes a plan to get everything back to being "all right" and then puts the plan into action. Of course, the bad guy/antagonist opposes the main character at every turn, but in most cases he, she, or it is eventually defeated in the *climax* (the height of the action or most exciting part).

In the resolution, all is well again in some way. It may be different from where the story started, and in our sin-cursed world, the stories we tell ourselves often reflect creation's brokenness through bittersweet endings. But the good stories—the ones we come back to—always have good somehow triumph at the end.

The classic tale of Cinderella is a good example of these elements. The story begins happily, with our protagonist (Cinderella) in the care of her loving parents. But then her mother dies (the inciting incident), and Cinderella must endure the persecution of her wicked stepmother (the antagonist). Cinderella's one hope for escaping her terrible circumstances is marrying her true love, the prince, so most of the story centers around her efforts to attend the palace ball (the rising action). The stepmother foils her every effort until the fairy godmother comes to help, and Cinderella attends the ball—but has to run away at midnight, leaving her slipper behind. The climax of the story occurs when the prince discovers that the shoe fits Cinderella. In the resolution, the two are married and all is well.

This is the basic format that most stories follow. But did you ever think about where this nearly universal structure came from? Why is *this* what makes a good story? Why can't we have a story without an antagonist? Why can't we just do away with the rising action and have everything turn out right immediately? Why does it always have to end well or at least with a little bit of hope?

The answer is that God is the greatest storyteller this world has ever known. He wrote the story of this world, and all our movies and novels are, consciously or subconsciously, patterned off of that one great story. At the level of basic structure, the stories we tell ourselves reflect reality—even if we don't realize it.[1]

THE BEGINNING OF TIME

Let's start where any good story starts—at the beginning.

Our fairy tales begin with, "Once upon a time." But the Bible begins at the very start of time, so perhaps it's better to simply use the words the Bible does: "In the beginning, God created the heavens and the earth" (Gen. 1:1).

We're told that in the beginning, the creation was "very good" (Gen. 1:31). Perfect. In our world groaning under sin's curse, we can't even imagine what that was like. It must have been full of vibrant color, dripping with the sweetness and goodness of the fruits and vegetables that grew naturally, without weed killer or bug spray. Great cats and dogs and birds with glorious plumage, all roaming about with no fear of man, woman, or each other.

Humans were the crowning jewel of God's creation. Of no other plant or animal did he say, "This one bears my image."

Man was supposed to represent God by ruling over this earth. He was supposed to have dominion over the plants and the animals.

Adam and Eve—the first man and woman—weren't just created for dominion, however. They were made for fellowship with God. They could speak with him and enjoy his presence. They could have a close, intimate relationship with their very Maker.

God made just one rule: they weren't to eat the fruit of one specific tree, the "tree of the knowledge of good and evil" (Gen. 2:17). The presence of this rule wasn't out of cruelty; it allowed Adam and Eve to show their love for God through obedience. It was an obedience that would never hurt them or even inconvenience them—they had every other tree in the garden to enjoy.

This was the setting: a perfect world, and mankind perfectly happy, in unbroken fellowship with a good and glorious God.

ENTER THE ANTAGONIST

The setting is described in Genesis 1 and 2. That perfection of bliss spans all of two chapters in the sixty-six books of the Bible.

Chapter 3 begins thus: "Now the serpent was more crafty than any beast of the field which the LORD God had made. He said to the woman, 'Did God actually say, "You shall not eat of any tree in the garden"?'" (v. 1). The serpent, of course, was not a mere animal. It was indwelt by Satan—the devil, the very first rebel—himself.

It began with a simple, seemingly innocent question. But it all went downhill from there. Just a few verses into this very odd conversation (was Eve not surprised that the serpent could *talk*?), the snake openly contradicted God's words.

"The serpent said to the woman, 'You will not surely die. For God knows that when you eat of it your eyes will be opened, and you will be like God, knowing good and evil'" (Gen. 3:4–5). God had said that if they ate of the tree, they would surely die (Gen. 2:17). The serpent said, "You will *not* die!" He called God a liar and painted him as a harsh master, determined to keep true enlightenment and happiness from his creatures.

The woman listened. So did her husband. They ate the fruit they had been commanded not to eat, and immediately they were filled with shame.

They had sinned. Their fellowship with God was broken. They had tried to rise to the level of gods and so fell. The perfect happiness they had enjoyed in obedience to their Creator was gone, replaced by the futile striving of pride and selfishness.

Death entered the world. The created order was cursed (Gen. 3:17–18; Rom. 8:19–22). Adam and Eve died a spiritual death in that moment, and a physical death would follow.

This is the inciting incident. The antagonist was the serpent—or rather, Satan who indwelt it. The perfect setting was smashed. The created order was turned on its head—man, who was supposed to rule the animals under God's authority, loosed himself from God's rule and submitted to an animal.

What's more, all of Adam's descendants share in that choice and its consequences. When we're born, we share Adam's sinful, dead, and dying nature. We come into this world as enemies of God—and he must punish us.

God is holy, the perfection and definition of goodness, completely set apart from anything opposed to his perfect nature. He can't stand evil. Humanity has offended against the infinitely beautiful and worthy Creator of all that exists, and, being just, God must punish that sin. As John Piper explains, if God were to refrain from punishing evil, "a lie would reign at the core of reality."[2]

THE PLAN AND THE RISING ACTION

God himself laid out the plan for restoration in Genesis 3:15: "I will put enmity between you [the serpent, or Satan] and the woman, and between your offspring and her offspring; he shall bruise your head, and you shall bruise his heel."

Somebody was going to come, one who was descended from Eve, and he would crush the head of the serpent—although he himself would be bruised on the heel. The heel is a painful place for a snakebite, but if you've ever tried to kill a snake, you know that a strike on the head is a deathblow for a serpent.

The entire Old Testament is the story of rising action as God slowly reveals more of his plan and begins to put all the pieces in place for the great offensive.

We watch as he chooses the nation of Israel to represent him on earth by ruling the other nations in obedience to him. We watch Israel fall into sin as they worship the false gods of the nations they were supposed to rule—obeying the heathen peoples just as Adam obeyed the serpent. We see God's plan of redemption for Israel as he allows the other nations to rule them for a while but promises that their perfect King is coming.

Slowly, one by one, the prophecies come to light. There's the promise to Abraham that all the nations will be blessed in him (Gen. 12:3). There's the Passover and all the animal sacrifices that could cover sins but never take them away, pointing to the once-for-all sacrifice that was coming (Heb. 10:4). There's Psalm 2, the prophecy that the Son of God, a great King, God's Anointed (Messiah, or Christ) was coming to rule all the nations who reject God—fulfilling what none of Israel's kings could do. And there's Isaiah 53, the almost-unbelievable description of the suffering that God's chosen one would undergo as the sacrifice for our sins.

The Old Testament is a story of waiting, even as God continues to reveal himself to Israel, uncover bits and pieces of his plan, and set the pieces in place on the chessboard of history. This is the bigger narrative that makes sense out of the individual histories of Joshua, Samson, David, Elijah, and all the others.

A BLOODY PLOT TWIST

Most epic fantasies and action movies feature a battle at their climax. Somebody has to die—the evil witch has to be killed, the mastermind of the plot to take over the world needs to be assassinated, the opposing army must be defeated.

Climaxes are often bloody. They also tend to feature an element of surprise—there's a plot twist, somebody turns out to be a double agent, a character you never expected to die is killed.

The climax of history, as recorded in the Bible, was bloody too. It was also very surprising—even though it had been foreshadowed and prophesied for centuries.

The Messiah, the coming Savior, the one who would rule over Israel as King and be the sacrifice for their sins, was coming. Israel was waiting. They'd been waiting for centuries. At this point, they were under the powerful hand of the Roman Empire, and they were desperate to break free. They were looking for their Messiah, hoping he would deliver them from Rome.

He didn't come like they expected.

He was born in a stable, to a virgin and her husband. The only men who honored his birth were poor shepherds and wealthy magi from another country, although an entire host of angels sang praises, and celestial events heralded his advent. The jealous puppet king of Israel had every young child in Bethlehem murdered when he heard of it. This was Messiah's welcome into the world.

He grew up as a carpenter and traveled the length of Israel as a humble teacher, essentially homeless. He ate with wealthy religious leaders and with the sinners they despised. He had the same care for high-ranking officials and lowly, disregarded women.

But he wasn't just a humble teacher. Again and again, he made the startling declaration that he was the Son of God. "I and the Father are one," he said (John 10:30). And again, "I am," which was the Old Testament name for God himself (John 8:58). He made very clear that he was the Messiah, the Son of the holy and eternal God, the one who had been promised throughout the Old Testament.

Jesus of Nazareth was God made man. J. I. Packer explains, "He was no less God then than before; but he had begun to be man."[3] The second person of the Trinity took a human nature to himself, walking among men while remaining perfectly sinless.

The Jewish leaders hated him. A humble rabbi, even an eccentric one, would have been acceptable, but not the Son of God. They had formed their own religious system, which gave them money and power and which could not stand the coming of the God they supposedly worshiped. And so, they conspired to have him killed.

The climax of all history was bloody. It was the blood of the main character, our world's Creator, dying on a cross (possibly the worst instrument of torture humanity has ever conceived). It was a surprise like no other—Israel was looking for a King to save them from Roman domination. The King died as a sacrificial lamb.

The salvation Israel was looking for was a military deliverance. What they really needed was deliverance from the holy, righteous wrath of God.

We deserve God's judgment. Jesus Christ, the God-man, took it on himself. He "[became] a curse for us" (Gal. 3:13), the curse that should fall on every one of us who has not kept every one of God's commands.

So his disciples watched in confusion as the sun went dark and the one they thought would deliver them hung dying, and as yet they didn't quite understand.

He cried out, "It is finished," and gave up his spirit (John 19:30). He died. But that wasn't the end.

SUNDAY: THE TRUE CLIMAX

If the story had ended on Friday, with the Messiah dead in a tomb, everything would have been finished. There would be no Christian faith. No gospel.

The disciples thought it was over. "We had hoped," they said, "that he was the one to redeem Israel" (Luke 24:21). But their hope had ended with their Lord's death—or so they believed.

Imagine their surprise, the disbelief, the dawning realization on Sunday morning, that *the tomb was empty*. That the one who had been quite dead was very much alive. Imagine their amazement when the angels declared, "He is risen!" When they saw him with their own eyes, and he ate fish in front of them to prove he wasn't a ghost (Luke 24:43).

This was the true climax of all history: when God incarnate, who died for the sins of the world, rose from the dead in mighty vindication. This is the ground of all our faith.

Christ became the second Adam. Unlike our first father, he kept every one of God's commands while he was here on earth. He obeyed the Father perfectly. And just like we all share in Adam's dead nature when we're born, when we trust in Christ—not our own works—to save us, we share in all his righteousness. He takes our punishment, and we take his perfection: "For as many of you as were baptized into Christ have put on Christ" (Gal. 3:27).

We could never have restored that fellowship with God on our own. No obedience, no rebellion or hard work, could ever save us. God did it all for us. Every verse of the Bible has to be read in light of this—Jesus Christ's life, death, and resurrection.

OUR PART IN THE STORY

And that leads us to the present day.

Forty days after his resurrection, Jesus ascended back into heaven. In his physical absence, he sent his Spirit to indwell believers, beginning with the apostles.

He gave the apostles a special charge: to make disciples of all nations (Matt. 28:19). They were to found the church, the community of those who put their faith in Christ Jesus for salvation.

The church is described as Jesus's body and his bride, and it will continue until the end times.

That's where we are today, in between the climax and the resolution. Jesus is not physically here, but his Spirit is. He works through his word to produce faith in our hearts, and then he lives within believers to sanctify us (make us more like Christ, more set apart from sin and the world).

We don't know exactly how long this part of the story will last. We do know that we should be "waiting for our blessed hope, the appearing of the glory of our great God and Savior Christ Jesus" (Titus 2:13), although we don't know when that will be. In the meantime, we have a clear mission—believe the word, be transformed by the word, and preach the word to others.

This is our part in the story. We're not the main character (that's God). We're not the villain (that's Satan, who's already been defeated and will one day be destroyed). We're God's creation, upon whom he has lavished unimaginable, rescuing love. It's no wonder the Psalms are filled with commands to "praise the Lord!"

A RESOLUTION AT THE END OF AGES

The last third of a book is usually the worst. Not that it's the worst written. It's the worst for the characters who inhabit it. Those last several chapters are where every possible trial and painful challenge is thrown at the characters.

What's worse, while we, the readers, know it's a story and the good guys are likely to win, the characters don't know that. As far as they're concerned, when that massive army comes charging or the monster attacks, it might be the end. They don't (usually) know the author who is designing every event to bring the story to a satisfying conclusion.

Jesus said that while we're on this earth, we'll have tribulation. We're promised that "all who desire to live a godly life in Christ

Jesus will be persecuted" (2 Tim. 3:12) because the world around us hates the truth of the Bible and wants to see it silenced. What's more, we live in a world that groans under the curse brought on it by sin. Hurricanes, earthquakes, tornadoes, and droughts are almost constantly in the news.

But we know the ending of the story. And it doesn't end like this.

Revelation 21 and 22 describe new heavens and a new earth. God will dwell among men, and his glory will be so bright there won't even be a need for the sun or moon. He'll wipe away every tear. We won't have any more suffering, death, or pain. Everything will be made new.

Remember how the resolution brings everything back to being good again? In the end, God's original design for his creation will be restored. And we Christians—those who have been saved by Jesus's blood and righteousness—will be there. We'll have perfect, unbroken fellowship with him, beholding his glory without ceasing.

That's the end of the story. And it's only the beginning.

QUESTIONS

1. Have you ever thought of the Bible as one big story before? In what ways is it helpful?

2. Why is it important that we look at every story, command, and promise in the Bible as part of the larger story? Does this change the way you think about the Bible?

3. What part of this great story is most encouraging or impactful to you? Why?

4

GOD'S WILL FOR MY LIFE

God's will for my life.

That's something we think about a lot as teens. It encompasses many questions: *Should I go to college? And where? What career should I pursue? Is it the right time for me to date? Is this the right person? Should I go down this path or seize that opportunity?*

Those questions are important, but they're just the surface. The real question is so much bigger. Beyond our queries about college and careers and relationships, we need to know God's will for our lives as a whole. What is God's design and purpose for us? What should our lives be about?

The Bible answers these questions.

As we study God's word, we get to learn our Creator's design for us and his purpose for our lives. This is such an important aspect of our Bible study—yet it's easy to misunderstand or approach it the wrong way. That's why, over the next two chapters, we'll be talking about how the Bible not only reveals God's will for us but also helps us live it out.

Before we get started, however, we need to define what we mean by "God's will." There are actually two different ways to use the term. The first refers to "God's sovereign governance of all that comes to pass."[1] We call this his *sovereign will*.

The other meaning of the term "God's will" is his *revealed will*. This is what he has told us to do, what he has commanded. It's his laws and rules.

As you've probably guessed, the second meaning is what we'll be discussing in this chapter. What has God told us to do? Why has he given us these commands? What is his design—his will—for our lives?

INTO HIS IMAGE

What is our Creator's purpose for us? Paul puts it clearly and succinctly:

> And we know that for those who love God all things work together for good, for those who are called *according to his purpose*. For those whom he foreknew he also predestined to *be conformed to the image of his Son, in order that he might be the firstborn among many brothers*. (Rom. 8:28–29)

God's purpose for us is that we would be conformed into his own image. Think of it! His purpose is that we would become *like him*. It is that Jesus Christ would be the first and greatest among a host of brothers and sisters who have been transformed into his likeness. And he *will* accomplish that purpose in us.

In Galatians 4:19, Paul expresses his earnest desire for "Christ [to be] formed in" his readers. Beyond just our words and actions, God's purpose for us is to be made like Christ at the level of our heart and mind.

We'll be discussing *how* that transformation takes place in the next chapter. For now, we're going to see *what* exactly that image looks like. What is it that we're being conformed to? For that purpose, we'll need to look at God's commands—what they are, why they're important, and why we study them.

We begin in the book of Exodus.

THUNDER FROM SINAI

The people of Israel were finally free from their four-hundred-year slavery in Egypt. God had performed incredible wonders to bring them out of their bondage, sending fierce plagues on Egypt's king and people. He had delivered his people from Pharaoh's army, leading them along the dry bottom of the Red Sea between quivering walls of water. He had miraculously provided food and water in the desert despite their constant complaining. Now they had come to a stop before Mount Sinai.

This was where God would speak to Israel. Here he would reveal his law, the decrees by which this chosen nation was to live. Thunderclouds, lightning, and the blast of an otherworldly trumpet atop the mountain marked his coming.

The last part of Exodus and most of Leviticus detail the laws God gave Moses for the nation of Israel at that mountain. Some were very minor and specific, like what to do if a person had leprosy or if somebody's cow got lost. Others gave instructions for cases of murder or kidnapping. Many dealt with the danger of idolatry—of God's people turning away from their Creator to find their hope in powerless idols.

At the very heart of all these decrees were the Ten Commandments. These are the central laws God himself wrote on two stone tablets. We still refer to them today. They're displayed in public places and private homes, and many of them form the basis for our civil law.

Why did God give his people all these commands? Was he merely trying to prove their loyalty? Or was there another, deeper reason?

THE HEART OF THE LAW

When Jesus was on earth, he was asked what was the greatest commandment in the law. He didn't cite any of the Ten Commandments. He didn't say it was "do not murder" or "do not commit adultery."

The greatest commandment, according to Jesus, is found in Deuteronomy 6: "Hear, O Israel: The LORD our God, the LORD is one. *You shall love the LORD your God* with all your heart and with all your soul and with all your mind" (vv. 4–5). Knowing his infinite goodness and beauty, God's people are to adore him and find joy being in his presence.

The second most important is found in Leviticus 19:18: "You shall love your neighbor as yourself." Rather than just keeping external rules about how to treat others, God's people are to love those around them from the heart and seek their good.

Jesus said that "on these two commandments depend all the Law and the prophets" (Matt. 22:40). All the commands of God boil down to these two rules: Love God with everything you have, and love the people around you as yourself.

The heart of God's law is love.

The Ten Commandments
Exodus 20:1-17

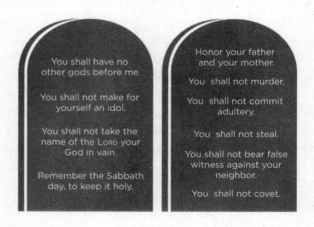

You shall have no other gods before me.

You shall not make for yourself an idol.

You shall not take the name of the LORD your God in vain.

Remember the Sabbath day, to keep it holy.

Honor your father and your mother.

You shall not murder.

You shall not commit adultery.

You shall not steal.

You shall not bear false witness against your neighbor.

You shall not covet.

"I am the LORD your God, who brought you out of the land of Egypt, out of the house of slavery." (Ex. 20:2)

Illustration 4.1: The Ten Commandments

THE HEART OF GOD

Before anything else, the law is a manifestation of God's character. It declares who he is. God, as the Creator, defines what is good and right. The law relates this in written form.

In the Ten Commandments (and all the rest of the law) we can see God's heart. He is the God of truth—therefore he commands we bear no false witness against our neighbor. He is a God of faithfulness—therefore, he forbids unfaithfulness to a wife or husband.

He is the God of justice—therefore, he made laws to guard against exploitation of the poor and of women. He forbade his people to mistreat one another, whether through theft, adultery, murder, or simply coveting each other's possessions.

He is the God of love—therefore, he commanded Israel to care for the orphan, the widow, and the alien (Deut. 10:18). He is the satisfaction of our souls—therefore, he commands that we not worship anything else or place our trust in anyone other than him.

Love is the heart of God's law because it is the heart of God.

When we read God's word, our instinct is to immediately look for rules to follow. And of course, we are to obey God's commands. However, we should first look for what they tell us about God. What aspects of his character are revealed? What do we learn about his justice, his truth, and his goodness?

The law, like the rest of the Bible, is not primarily about us but about God.

FOR OUR BENEFIT

However, while the law isn't all about us, it is for us. It's a set of commands we were meant to keep.

As Pastor Tim Keller explains, keeping the law was promised to lead to flourishing. It's not a set of arbitrary decrees. Because we were made in God's image, breaking the law not only goes against his nature—it goes against ours.[2]

If you think about it, it makes sense. Laws against stealing, murder, or unfaithfulness in marriage feel *right* to us. They fit with the moral blueprint God has put in our hearts as beings made in his image. A civilization that accepted the evils that God's law prohibits would strike us as absurd.

What's more, we know that breaking these laws doesn't end well. We've seen the consequences over and over—broken people, broken relationships, broken societies.

Keeping the law leads to healthy families and communities. But God's law isn't just about practical or social issues—it's not just there to tell us how to get along better or create a utopian society. If that was all, we could get along quite well without the Bible. We would only need the government or one of any number of other religious systems to tell us what to do.

We have a deeper need than physical and social flourishing. Made in God's image, at the core of our nature, we need *him*.

THE ONLY SOURCE OF FULFILLMENT

We were designed for fellowship and communion with God. This is stunning. The infinite, eternal being who created us wants us to have *fellowship* with him?

In fact, we were so created that we can *only* be fulfilled in God. All our desires for intimacy, for fulfillment, all our desires to be known and seen, can only be satisfied through a relationship with our Maker. We can seek to fulfill those desires in this world through money, popularity, friendship, romance, or achievements, but in the end all those things will fall short and we'll be left looking for more.

As we saw, the first, greatest, and central commandment is to love God with everything we have. This isn't the unreasonable whim of a tyrant. It's the gracious command of a God who more than deserves all our love and will satisfy our souls like nothing and no one else ever can.

John Piper has famously said, "God is most glorified in us when we are most satisfied in him."[3] God created us for his glory (Isa. 43:7). Our purpose is to make him known, to ascribe all worth to him, and to reflect his glory. We don't do that by a grudging obedience to his commands. We do that by finding our greatest joy in him—because then we make him known as the most beautiful, satisfying thing in the universe.

If we're finding our joy in God, then we'll naturally follow the second command to love our neighbors as ourselves. It should be the outflow of an overwhelming satisfaction in God. If our joy is found in God, we don't *need* to steal from our neighbor to be happy because we already have all we need in God. If we're confident in God's love, we won't get angry when things don't go our way because we know he has our ultimate good in mind.

This is the point of the law: that we should find our satisfaction in God and love those around us, all for his glory. The law is not a call to arduous drudgery. It's a call to love and joy.

IT'S ALL ABOUT FAITH

Where does this kind of love come from? John Piper explains, "The origin of love is the heart of faith."[4] In other words, if we're going to truly *love* God (and as a result, those around us), we have to *trust* him.

This is illustrated in the Ten Commandments. God preceded the commands with a ringing statement about himself: "I am the LORD your God, who brought you out of the land of Egypt, out of the house of slavery" (Ex. 20:2). The Israelites' motivation for obedience was to be: the knowledge of who God was (their eternal, powerful God), what he had done for them (delivered them from slavery!), and what he had promised to do (give them a beautiful, fertile country).

Knowing God, and knowing what he had done and promised, they were to trust that he was good—better than all the idols they tried to worship. That trust in him would lead to obedience and love, just like we love and obey our parents when we trust that they love us and only have our best interests in mind.

As New Testament believers, we have yet more reason to trust and obey our God—we can look back at Jesus's life, death, and resurrection, and to the "living hope" (1 Pet. 1:3) at the end of the story, and see his goodness, faithfulness, and love. This is our motivation for obedience: faith in what God has done and what he's promised to do.

The law called for complete trust in God, which would lead to love and obedience. Did the Israelites possess such faith? Do we?

GOLD LOOKED MORE LOVELY

While Moses was up on the mountain receiving the Ten Commandments from God himself, the Israelite people became restless. In the absence of their leader, they convinced Aaron (Moses's brother and right-hand man) to make them a golden calf to worship.

In the face of the thunderclouds that still rested atop Sinai, while Moses was speaking to God himself, the people venerated an idol and declared, "These are your Gods, O Israel, who brought you up out of the land of Egypt!" (Ex. 32:4). Just weeks before, God had displayed awesome power in delivering them, and every morning, they were receiving miraculous food. They knew better than to worship idols. Yet they decided a golden cow looked more lovely than their God.

When Moses came down from the mountain, the people were punished severely. And yet this was not the last time they would brazenly disobey God's law and fail to put their trust in him.

Throughout the wilderness journey, they grumbled and complained, although God provided everything they needed. They refused to enter the promised land because they feared the militant inhabitants, even though the almighty God had promised to fight with them. They rebelled against Moses, worshiped idols, and routinely ignored both God's provision and his punishments.

Under Moses, the Israelites never obeyed the law.

A RECORD OF FAILURE

Perhaps it was just that generation. They had been raised in Egypt among multitudes of idols. They hadn't grown up seeing God's glory in a cloud by day and a pillar of fire at night. Perhaps their children would obey as they had not.

During the lifetime of Joshua, Moses's successor, Israel did mostly follow the law. But after that, it went downhill—fast. The book of Judges is a frustrating history of cycles: God's people put their trust in idols and flagrantly disobey; God sends punishment in the form of other nations; Israel repents and cries to God; God sends them a deliverer, and the people worship God—until the deliverer dies. And . . . repeat.

In fact, the entire history of the Old Testament is a record of God's people failing to trust him and follow his law. It's true, there are bright spots. God-fearing kings such as David, Josiah, and Hezekiah stand in sharp relief against the dreary background of their depraved counterparts. But even they failed, David most famously with Bathsheba. The rest of Israel's and Judah's kings openly defied God, worshiping idols and even offering their own children on altars to false gods.

Over and over, God's prophets condemned Israel's sin and idolatry—but Israel didn't listen. They fell further and further into sin until God allowed them to be conquered and exiled by other nations.

The history of the Old Testament is almost painful to read. It's frustrating—why couldn't God's people obey? Why couldn't they just realize that they would only flourish, both physically and spiritually, when they were trusting and following God?

We can't just blame Israel, though. We're the exact same way. The entire human race is set against God. The moment we examine our own hearts and lives, we see the same idolatry, the same sin and darkness, within ourselves.

Over and over, we put our trust in God's gifts instead of himself. We look to money, friends, or entertainment to make us happy. If we know God, his Spirit will convict us, and we'll repent and turn to worship him—until we fall again. Each of our lives becomes another paragraph in this ages-old record of failure.

No human in the history of this world—save Jesus—has ever kept God's law. We're born hating him, as fundamentally opposed as dark is to light. We've broken every single commandment; we've sought satisfaction in everything else, and his image in us is fractured and twisted. That fellowship and love we were supposed to have with our Creator is broken and gone.

We can never, no matter how hard we try, measure up to his standard of perfect goodness and truth.

BEHOLD, THE LAMB OF GOD!

In the history of our world, only one human has ever been born who was not depraved, wicked, and a hater of God from the moment of conception. Jesus Christ, born of a virgin, fully God and yet fully man, came to do God's will (Heb. 10:7).

He shared in our flesh and blood and temptations. Hebrews says that he "in every respect has been tempted as we are, yet without sin" (Heb. 4:15). There is no temptation we face—idolatry, lust, fear, bitterness, pride—that he did not face and overcome. He trusted completely in his Father, and never once did his faith waver. He never once sinned.

The law that we couldn't keep, that was forever and infinitely out of our reach, he kept perfectly. And through his death and resurrection, that righteousness is counted as ours.

As we study God's commandments throughout the Bible, we need to keep this in mind. We could never keep those commandments on our own. We fail again and again. But Jesus Christ has kept them for us. "For as many of you were baptized into Christ have put on Christ" (Gal. 3:27). This is the doctrine of justification. All of Jesus's perfection, his perfect obedience, is made ours. When the Father looks at us, he sees Christ.

So when you, Christian, fall into the sin of anger and bitterness toward a sibling, parent, or friend, remember that Christ loved those around him to the very end—even the mother who never quite understood, the friend who denied him, and the disciple who betrayed his life.

When you've had an opportunity to share the good news of the gospel but hung back for fear of what people would think, remember that Christ endured scoffing and so much worse for your sake, and he never once turned aside.

When you've been thinking, speaking, and acting as though you're better than those around you, remember that Jesus took the position of a humble servant toward those who should have been kissing his feet.

And that is how our God sees us: covered by Jesus's blood and his righteousness.

LAW-KEEPER TURNED CHRIST-FOLLOWER

The apostle Paul had been the "perfect" Jew.

He kept every one of the basic rules and went beyond. He was a "Hebrew of Hebrews" (Phil. 3:5). He was a Pharisee, part of a group that devoted their lives to keeping every letter of the law. He even went so far as to say he was "blameless" in keeping the law (Phil. 3:6). In fact, he was so zealous for his religion that he persecuted the fledgling Christian church, pursuing its members and throwing them in prison—even looking on while they were killed (Acts 7:58; 8:1–3).

Talk about extra.

But when he became a Christian, he realized none of that frantic law-keeping mattered. He actually said it was all "loss"—garbage, dung (Phil. 3:7).

Paul realized something absolutely vital: we can never be saved by keeping the law. That won't get us closer to God. Instead, he found something far better.

> Indeed, I count everything as loss because of the surpassing worth of knowing Christ Jesus my Lord. For his sake I have suffered the loss of all things and count them as rubbish, in order that I may gain Christ and be found in him, *not having a righteousness of my own that comes from the law, but that which comes through faith in Christ*, the righteousness from God that depends on faith. (Phil. 3:8–9)

The only way we can ever be righteous is if Christ keeps the law for us and clothes us in his perfect obedience. But that leads us to another question. If we couldn't keep the law, and Christ has kept it for us perfectly, then why is it important for us today? Should we study it? And if so, how?

DOES THE LAW MATTER FOR CHRISTIANS?

In his letter to the church at Galatia, Paul rebuked the believers there for trying to go back to keeping the law in order to be saved. He also explained the very important role the law plays in our salvation:

> Therefore the Law has become our tutor to lead us to Christ, so that we may be justified by faith. (Gal. 3:24 NASB)

The law shows us our sin. It dramatically highlights the contrast between our depravity and God's holiness. It shows us that we are bad, and God alone is good. And it also shows us that we can't ever work hard enough or do enough good to be righteous enough to merit God's acceptance. No matter how hard we try, we will never live up to that perfect standard. Even if we look perfect on the outside and keep all the rules (like Paul), we're still sinful on the inside. We still love other things more than God. We're still born into Adam's dead nature.

And once we realize how sinful we are and how hopeless the task of trying to follow God's law is, we're ready to acknowledge our need of a Savior.

That's the first role of the law in the Christian's life. It shows us that we need a Savior. It won't stop reminding us how sinful we are until it drives us to Christ.

GRATEFUL OBEDIENCE

But what about after that? Jesus kept the law for us—we didn't have to do anything! Should we just forget about it now and do our own thing?

Again, Paul answers our question: "By no means! How can we who died to sin still live in it?" (Rom. 6:2).

Before we were saved, we could not keep God's law. We were actually slaves to sin (Rom. 6:17). But now that we're in Christ, we've been freed from that vile mastery. Instead, we're "slaves [to] righteousness" (Rom. 6:18)—an arrangement that results in life and joy as God's grace gives us the ability to obey him.

Before, we tried to obey out of fear and pride. Now, we obey out of love and gratitude. We don't have to be afraid of God's judgment; that already fell on Christ. He's made us new, given us a new heart, and put his Spirit inside us. So although we know we won't obey perfectly, we're able to love him and obey him out of joy and through faith in what he's done for us. And all the while, he is conforming us into his image, gradually making us more and more like Jesus Christ—all for his glory and our joy.

The law, then, is still important for us as Christians. It's not there because we need to keep it in order for God to love us.

Keeping it better won't make him love us more—he already loves each of us as he loves his Son, in whose perfect obedience we're clothed, and that love is infinite. He can't love us more because we can't get any bigger than infinity, and he'll never love us less because he doesn't change. Our obedience (or lack thereof) won't change his love.

Rather, the law shows us what it looks like to live in gratitude and love for God. The rules that were specific to the nation of Israel (such as the laws about property lines or marrying your dead brother's wife) no longer apply to Christians. But the moral law (summarized in the Ten Commandments and showing us God's character) still does, and it's reiterated throughout the New Testament.

In fact, most of the New Testament epistles spend significant time expounding the moral law. They give detailed descriptions of how we should live in light of the gospel. They give instructions for how the church should act: in love and unity, confessing and forgiving sin, showing hospitality, being faithful to one's spouse, and not showing partiality or discriminating on the basis of race or class.

HIS WILL FOR OUR LIVES

And so now we come back to our question from the beginning of the chapter: *What is God's will for our lives?*

It's that we would glorify him as we find satisfaction in him alone and love the people around us. It's that we would have faith in his person and promises so that love would flow from a trusting heart. It's that we would become more like him, "transformed into the same image from one degree of glory to another" (2 Cor. 3:18), conformed to his character as it's revealed in his law.

As we pursue this first, great purpose, we'll be able to address the other questions—such as whom we should marry or what career we ought to pursue. The answers may not always be easy, but when we're seeking to follow God with all that we are, we'll be in a position to make wise decisions. What's more, we'll know that all these choices are serving our primary purpose of being made more and more like Christ.

Because we're human and, even as Christians, we still have a sin nature inside us, we won't fulfill that purpose perfectly. Our lives and our relationships will still be broken and marred by our own sin. But we trust in the perfect righteousness of Christ that's been made ours, and we wait for the day when we'll finally be free.

WHY WE STUDY THE LAW

So why and how do we study the law? The Bible is full of exhortations and commands. We can't just skip those sections—we need to take them seriously and study them, but not so we can be a better Christian, improve our lives, or get God to love us.

As we've seen in this chapter, there are (at least) three good reasons to study the law of God:

- To learn more about him
- To make us thankful for his grace
- To show us what a grateful life looks like

We study the law first *to learn more about God*, so we can grow in our relationship with him. As we discussed above, the commands God has given us reveal his character. As we study his law, we can get to know him more. We see who he is through his commands.

The law also makes us *thankful for God's grace* by showing us how much we need Christ. We couldn't have saved ourselves. We couldn't have reached that standard on our own. Seeing how holy God is and how far from that standard we are should make us thankful for what Christ has done.

Lastly, the law shows us what it looks like to *live in gratitude to Christ*. As we study the commands of both the Old and New

71

Why?

Testaments, we'll see the blueprint of what our lives should look like—the image into which God is conforming us. We discover more and more about his character, which is to be reflected in our hearts, words, and actions.

But if we're such weak, sinful human beings—even after being saved—how can we ever hope to keep any of those commands? How are we going to be conformed into Christ's image when we still sin almost every chance we get? That's what we'll discuss in the next chapter.

QUESTIONS

1. Why is it important for us to study God's commands? What can we learn from them? How do they teach us about God?

2. Trying to keep God's commands to earn his favor is called *legalism*. Have you ever seen this in your own life? How does the truth of the gospel help you to fight it?

3. The law presents us with a standard we can't possibly reach on our own—the standard of God's own character. But Jesus has kept this standard for us. Spend some time in meditation or discussion on this beautiful truth. What difference does this make in your walk with Christ?

5

HOW TO OBEY GOD'S WILL

God's word commands our obedience. It's not a suggestion or a self-help book. It's the command of a sovereign, Creator God, and it's the only path to true joy and fulfilling our purpose.

But it's one thing for us to say God's commands are good and perfect and should be obeyed. It's quite another thing for us to actually obey them.

Obeying God's law does not come naturally to any of us. Since Adam's sin, our hearts are in rebellion against God. Our faces are set in direct opposition to his will. We want what we want—not what God wants. And even though as Christians we've been made new in Christ, we still have to battle against that old nature every day. Obedience still doesn't come naturally.

If you don't believe it, think about the last time someone mistreated you. Maybe it was a tiny annoyance or maybe it was a major betrayal of trust. Either way, did you immediately feel great love and forgiveness toward that person?

Probably not. More likely you wanted to yell or throw out some barbed remark to indicate what a terrible person he or she was. In moments like those, we desperately want to ignore commands like "love your enemy" and "forgive those who have wronged you."

Not only that, the world around us *tells* us to feel this way. *You have rights. You deserve your space and your stuff.* The messages we hear through the media every day don't usually encourage us to be humble or to find joy in something bigger than ourselves and our possessions.

The messages of the world, the temptations of the devil, and the desires of our own sin nature are like a rushing river that's constantly pulling us toward sin. If we let ourselves drift and just go with the flow, we'll choose evil every time. Following God means swimming upstream—fighting the current of that powerful river.

Obedience requires a mighty defiance of everything within ourselves and every message the world throws at us.

Obedience requires a lot more than we have.

THE HARD THING OF HEART CHANGE

What makes this so hard is that it's not just about following a lot of rules. Anyone can do that. If we're armed with enough fear of failure or enough incentive, we'll keep superficial rules down to the tiniest detail. That's what every other religious system is—a list of rules you have to keep if you want to be blessed or go to heaven. That was the religion of the Pharisees in Jesus's day, and it's the religion of millions today.

And we want Christianity to be that way too. We have proud hearts that want to boast in our own accomplishments. We want to trust in ourselves and think we can be good enough to please God. We would never say it out loud, but we like to think, *Look how much I've done! I'm the perfect Christian. I deserve for God to love me.*

So we make lists for ourselves—how long our devotions need to be, how we should dress, the words we should use (and of course, we would *never* do any "big" sins like murder or stealing).

And we tell ourselves that if we follow all those rules, we're doing okay.

But obedience to God isn't about rule-following. It's about a changed heart.

Remember what we talked about in the last chapter? The point of the law is that we should love God and find all our fulfillment in him. We should seek what's best for those around us, even when it hurts. It goes so much deeper than our external actions and words.

This is what Jesus was talking about in the Sermon on the Mount. The Pharisees had perfected the art of keeping every single external commandment in the law. *We need to give God a tenth of all our crops? Okay, let's make sure we even give a tenth of these tiny little spices* (Matt. 23:23). *No work on the Sabbath day? All right, let's make a rule about how far people can walk on the Sabbath, just to be extra sure.* And yet Jesus called these men "whitewashed tombs" (Matt. 23:28). Why? Because their hearts were just as black as anyone else's.

Jesus called for a much more radical obedience. In the Sermon on the Mount, he penetrated to the heart of God's commands to deal with the *attitudes* that lead to our actions. We might think we're doing pretty well on not murdering anybody, for instance—until we realize that our murderous, angry thoughts make us just as guilty in God's eyes. Not killing anybody or stealing their belongings isn't enough; we need to love them, be kind to them, forgive them, and genuinely seek their best.

We might think that as long as we go to church faithfully, pray, read the Bible, and evangelize, we're doing all right with our Christian life, but God calls for us to love him with everything we have, seek his glory in everything we do, and find our joy in him alone.

More than zealous rule-followers, our Father wants zealous Christ-followers. He wants us to *become* more like his Son.

POWER WE DON'T HAVE

We can't do that. We don't naturally love God—we love this world, and we love ourselves. And when you're surrounded by things you can see and feel and taste, it's hard to trust an invisible God. We're powerless to follow him.

But he hasn't left us to ourselves. He is the source of the power we don't have, and he graciously offers it to us.

We could study the fruit of the spirit (Gal. 5:22–23) all day, and never make any progress with it. But we'd be missing the entire point—that it's the fruit of the *Spirit*. It's a result of the Spirit's work inside us.

God is omnipotent, all-powerful. And the same God who created the earth, caused a worldwide deluge, and makes sure our planet rotates at just the right speed, is *inside* us. That same God is working in us to kill our sin and gradually make us more like himself.

But how does it work? It's not a magical process—we don't wake up one morning to find ourselves suddenly more patient with our family and friends, more humble and willing to forgive.

More to the point of our purpose here, how does Scripture fit into this picture? Merely reading or studying God's commandments doesn't mean we'll automatically follow them. It may only lead to discouragement as we realize how powerless we are to obey.

But what if the Bible doesn't just give us commands to obey— what if it actually helps us follow them?

A QUEST FOR TRUE JOY

If the point of obedience is a changed heart that takes more delight in God than in self or stuff, then it makes sense that we should begin at the heart level, with a quest for true joy. That means we should be growing in our faith, and, as a result, in love for God (as we talked about in the last chapter).

But . . . how?

If you've grown up in church or been a Christian for a while, you *know* that you should love God, that you should pursue intimacy with him and satisfaction in him alone. You know you should believe what he says and trust his promises even when things get rough. That sounds beautiful in theory—and it is beautiful—but where we get stuck is in trying to live it out.

We can try all kinds of things in this pursuit of joy. You might seek to get closer to God through being a really good Christian. You read your Bible every day and maybe devotionals or other Christian books as well. You go to church two or three times a week and volunteer for some of the different ministries. In fact, you may be just like I was as a young teen—looking like the perfect Christian on the outside and full of doubt and lack of love for God on the inside.

Or you can try to have an emotional experience that will fix your lack of love for God. It could be a camp, a worship night at your church, a revival meeting, or a Christian concert. Those things are good—just like reading your Bible and volunteering for ministries is good—but the emotional high is just that: a high. It doesn't last. It can even lead to discouragement as you go back to "normal life" and realize you can't maintain that emotion for very long.

You might even try to conjure up joy and love with your own willpower—just think hard enough, and you'll love God more. But it doesn't take long to realize that doesn't work very well either.

FIGHTING FOR FAITH

We need something more. We need something more than we can achieve on our own, more than our culture offers, more than mere emotion.

We need faith.

The word *faith* is thrown around a lot: "Just have faith," or "We just need a little faith." Christians and unbelievers alike know faith is important—how often have you seen the word *Believe* emblazoned on a backpack or t-shirt? But what we often miss is that faith needs an object. You put your trust *in* something or someone.

You might have heard that sincerely believing something—anything—is enough. But that doesn't even match up with what we know from everyday life. I can believe as firmly as I want that there's food in the fridge (you know—snack food, not salad food), but that doesn't help me when I look inside and discover my mom hasn't gone grocery shopping yet. What matters more than the size of our faith is the trustworthiness of its object.

What's more, our faith grows according to how trustworthy we know its object to be. If I climb up to a tree house, I may not trust it very much. I don't care for heights anyway, and what if it wasn't built well? What if it breaks? But if my dad is there, and he tells me he built that tree house, then I'll trust it a lot more. I know my dad is an engineer, and if he built something, it'll hold. My faith in the tree house grows once I know it's trustworthy.

God is the ultimately worthy object of our faith. He is the Creator of all the other things in which we put our trust. He is sovereign over every event, every person, every atom on this earth, and he is perfectly good, loving, and righteous. If we put our trust in tree houses, how much more should we trust our Maker? How much more should we trust that he loves us, his law is perfect, everything he does is good, we are saved through the blood of his Son, and every one of his promises will be fulfilled?

TRUST AND OBEY

Faith, as we discussed earlier, leads to obedience and love.

How will we love God if we don't really believe he's all that great? How can we see him as more desirable than any of the idols our hearts chase after if we don't trust that he's perfectly good?

We know our God is good, loving, just, kind, all-powerful, holy, merciful, and everything we need. We know these things, and we would affirm them with our lips, but do we really believe them deep in our hearts? Is this belief strong enough to direct our thinking and feeling, our words and our actions?

We need ever-greater faith. We need a heart that's being transformed to trust God and love him with everything we have. We need to be so confident of our acceptance by God that we don't try to find identity in the praise of others or the number of likes we get on social media. We need to trust that the reward waiting for us is better than anything this earth can offer, so we don't become envious when our friends or siblings get something we want.

We need to have faith that God is really in control of every nation and politician, and that he is a righteous and just God, so we don't become discouraged, bitter, and fearful at all the injustice that happens in this world every single day.

God is worthy of that trust—completely, unquestionably worthy. And yet, we find our faith is weak, and we're easily swayed. We succumb to doubt and despair far too easily. The size of our faith doesn't match the greatness of the God we serve. How can we change this? How can we grow in our faith and develop a deep-seated trust and confidence in God?

If the size of our faith grows in proportion to how trustworthy we know its object to be, we need to understand just how worthy of trust our God really is. We need to see his power and his goodness. We need to dwell on his greatness, his glory, and the gospel, and meditate on his promises. We need to see him for who he is, and as we understand more and more how worthy he is of all trust, our faith in him will grow.

GROWING IN LOVE

We saw earlier that the heart of the law is love—first for God, and then for others. If faith leads to obedience, then it must lead to love. But this, like faith, can seem elusive.

A few years back, I was gradually becoming aware that I didn't love God like I should. I saw other people who seemed to take great joy in reading their Bible. I could see they had a passion for God and his glory that I didn't. I thought about the gospel, the incredible love of God, and the sacrifice of Jesus Christ, and I was ashamed that I barely even felt grateful for what God had done.

So I tried to make myself feel love for God. Late at night, when I couldn't sleep, I tried as hard as I could to muster up joy and thankfulness. I sang the songs in youth group and hoped they would make me feel the passion I was missing. I tried to create love for God within my own heart.

It didn't work. I wondered if there was something wrong with me, or if I was even saved at all. *If I was a real Christian, wouldn't I love God more?*

What I didn't realize was, that's not how love works. The problem wasn't that I didn't try hard enough. *It was that I didn't know my God well enough.*

Think about your best friend. How did your relationship get to that level? How did you get to the point where you enjoy someone so much that you would do a lot just to be able to hang out? You probably didn't just decide, "This person will be my best friend." Friendships happen when you spend time with people. You get to know them. You learn how they think, what they like and dislike, what drives them, and how they react to tough situations.

This is how our hearts work. We can't just force ourselves to feel love. The people or things we love inspire it in our hearts through their goodness or inherent worth. We don't usually feel great love for snakes or stinging insects. We don't (naturally, apart from God's help) love nasty, obnoxious people.

God, on the other hand, is infinitely worthy of our love. He is worthy of more affection and joy than the human heart even has the capacity to hold. He is perfectly good, unendingly beautiful, and full of splendor. He is God, Yahweh, the one who does not change and always fulfills his word. He is awesome and full of majesty, a king who makes earth itself tremble, and yet who is more gentle than the kindest father with his newborn child. He is holy, a fearsome, righteous Judge, and yet he is so full of love toward his creation that he would send his own Son to die in our place.

This is the God who commands us to love him and promises to satisfy our every desire.

LEARN TO KNOW YOUR GOD

Do you see how love for God—the heart of all he's commanded us—requires faith? We need to trust in what he's told us about himself, and that leads us to love him. But to trust and love God, we need to *know* him.

We can't love God and find our delight in him if he remains a far-off, theoretical being, a subject for intelligent conversation and nothing else. Nor can we love him if we never devote any time or energy to learning about him. It's hard to trust and love someone you barely know. We have to behold him, learn more about him, spend time with him, and experience his grace.

That's what we seek to do in Bible study.

Bible study isn't just about gaining a bunch of knowledge. It's not about becoming a better Christian so God will love you more (the Lord forbid we ever think that way!). It's not about being smarter so we can feel better about ourselves. In fact, if all we ever do is collect information about God without letting it touch our hearts and move us to love and wonder, we've completely missed it.

In Bible study, we get to behold our God. His word is how he's revealed himself to us, and as we study it, we get to immerse ourselves in the vast ocean of discovering who he is. Our finite, created minds can hardly begin to fathom his infinity, and yet he invites us to climb up on his lap, as it were, and listen to him tell us about himself.

This is how we get to know the Lord and Creator of the universe. This is how we acquaint ourselves with who he is, so we'll grow in our trust and love for him.

And this kind of love is what manifests itself in obedience to him. Our obedience to the commands and exhortations in his word can be nothing other than the outflow of our love for the giver of those laws.

THE INVISIBLE PROCESS

We have a mango tree in our backyard. It's been there for as long as I can remember. Some years it produces fruit, and some years it doesn't.

My dad recently pruned off a bunch of branches that had died during the winter. It was as if most of the tree was gone; it looked barren. If you had watched it for a few days, you wouldn't have seen anything happening, and you might have assumed it was dead. But now it's been several weeks, and from my window, I can see that those dead-looking branches are covered with bright green leaves.

Like the growth of a tree, our sanctification—our growth into Christ's likeness—happens slowly, imperceptibly, invisibly. Timothy Keller reminds us that "growth in these graces . . . is very, very gradual."[1] It's rarely in leaps and bounds. Usually it happens by millimeters rather than inches, transformation taking place in the boring, the normal, the difficulties of everyday life—cleaning, school, work, and relationships.

God isn't confined to big acts of grace. He doesn't only work in major life events or pivotal experiences. His transforming power is just as present in the countless unnoticed, mundane moments of life. His grace is working every day as you open your Bible and come back to the same passage you've been studying for days or weeks.

Change comes slowly but so surely. The Spirit is the one who works in the hearts of our Father's children, and his work does not fail.

It won't always feel like it. You'll have seasons of great joy, but there are also seasons of dryness and great difficulty. And our God is still working. Just as you don't notice the stars as they pop out one by one against the blackness of night, but then you look up and see a galaxy, his truth is ever so gradually transforming our hearts.

TAKE UP THE CHALLENGE

This is why we study the Bible. If you picked up this book and wondered why someone would devote an entire book to Bible study, if you wondered why anyone would get so passionate about something that sounds like schoolwork—this is why. The Bible is not just another book. It's not inherently magical or mystically powerful, but it isn't ordinary either. It's how our Creator chose to communicate himself to us. That makes it essential.

We've just spent five chapters talking about why Bible study is so important. We might want to get straight to the practical, but it's important that we build a paradigm within which to pursue serious Bible study—otherwise we'll come at it with the wrong motivations, and eventually, when it gets hard, we'll get distracted or fall away.

But in the next part, we're going to dive into the immensely practical: *How do you study your Bible? And when? What tools should you use?* My prayer is that these next few chapters will equip you to start—or continue—on this journey of knowing and loving God more than you ever have before.

Yes, it's going to seem boring sometimes. You're going to wonder why you should read that chapter *again*, or why you need to make so many lists. You may think it feels like English class.

Can I encourage you, my friend? Don't give up. It may feel boring, but God is working where we can't see. His word is living, active, and sharper than a two-edged sword (Heb. 4:12). It pierces our hearts and changes us at the deepest core of our being. It's a book, but it's more than a book. It's the word of God himself.

Will you come with me? Will you take up the challenge? It's going to be tough, but it is so worth it. It is worth the sacrifice of time to draw nearer to our God. It is worth the hard work to let God's word sink deep into our hearts and change the way we think and feel and love. It is worth everything to be transformed by truth.

QUESTIONS

1. Why do we always gravitate toward lists and rules? How is the heart change that God promises to work in us harder than following rules? How is it better?

2. Have you felt the futility of trying to obey in your own strength? What have you done about it? Have you realized that it's God's power at work in us—not our own—that allows us to obey him? What might change in your thinking if you do realize this?

3. What are you doing to pursue the knowledge of God in your own life? What changes might you need to make? As we move into a discussion of the practical aspects of Bible study, what is your goal?

PART 2

HOW?

6

PART OF YOUR LIFE

What's the right time of day to study your Bible?

Depending whom you ask, you might get a lot of different answers. Some would say you absolutely must spend time in God's word first thing in the morning. Others would contend it's best to do it right before bed. I've heard speakers and teachers issue motivational challenges to very specific plans and schedules, such as committing to read your Bible for thirty minutes right after you get up each morning.

I don't know about you, but sometimes those kinds of challenges can foster legalism in my heart. If I don't spend the right amount of time reading or studying at the right time each day, I get discouraged. And if I do spend my allotted number of minutes in the word, then I feel great about myself—even if I wasn't focused on God or only did it out of pride.

That's not to say schedules and specific challenges are a bad thing at all. They're good and helpful in their place. But we shouldn't take them as divinely inspired. Nowhere in the Bible does God command a specific time each day when we should read his word. There's no verse that says, "Thou shalt study thy Bible at seven o'clock in the morning."

Instead, he gives us a broader—and more difficult—command. He calls us to let his word abide in us (John 15:7), to hide it in our hearts (Ps. 119:11), and to behold his glory (2 Cor. 3:18).

This frees us from being bound to one specific way of doing things. However, it also means we have a higher and harder task. Rather than merely devoting a specific number of minutes to the Bible each day, we need to cultivate a love for God's word. We need to view it as our lifeline, our anchor, the source of water to quench the thirst of our souls.

We need to make it our priority.

Just take a look at how different people in the Bible valued God's word:

- Moses commanded Israel to let God's words to them be *on their hearts*. They were to teach these words to their children and talk about them *at all times of the day* (Deut. 6:6–7).
- The psalmist meditated on God's word during the *night watches* (Ps. 119:148).
- The Israelites who returned from exile begged that God's word be read to them, and Ezra read it aloud for *several hours* at a time (Neh. 8:1–3).
- The early church *devoted themselves* to the apostles' teaching (Acts 2:42).
- The Bereans examined the scriptures *daily* to see if what Paul said about Jesus Christ was true (Acts 17:11).

When something is our priority, we'll do everything we can to make it happen. So if studying the Bible is our priority, we'll set aside time to do it. That may look different for different people, but the heart will be the same: making time to dig into God's word.

WHAT WORKS FOR ME?

The way this plays out in your own life will depend on the season and circumstances God has you in right now.

Do you have time in the morning (or could you make time by getting up earlier)? Or do you have to leave home early every day? Does the quiet of the evening work better, or do you have responsibilities then? Is the best time in the middle of the day, during a study hall or lunch break?

While we're not necessarily tied to a specific schedule, a routine is very helpful. How many times have you tried to form a new habit, only to have it fall by the wayside after a couple of weeks because you kept procrastinating or forgetting? If you have a time of day set aside for Bible study—whether that's before breakfast, during your lunch break, or just before bed—you're more likely to remember and do it.

For me, the best time is right after I get up. Part of it is habit—I've been doing it for so long that I can't imagine *not* reading and studying my Bible first thing in the morning. I also know that if I leave it until later in the day, other things will crowd it out. The biggest reason, though, is that if I don't spend time in God's word and prayer before I launch into the day, I find myself stuck in bad attitudes or snapping at my family. Your day might look different than mine, but it's still a good idea to spend a few minutes praying and meditating on Scripture when you get up—as well as throughout the day (Deut. 6:6–7).

Remember that studying the Bible is a habit, and forming habits takes time. If you miss doing it one day, don't give up. Just start again tomorrow (this is another way a schedule is helpful—it helps to make Bible study a fixed part of your day, so even when you do forget, you can come back to it easily).

Spending time in God's word is one of the most important habits you will ever form. It may also be one of the hardest. Remember how the world, the devil, and our flesh work against

Bible study? That battle starts right here—at the most basic level of sitting down to do it in the first place.

Schedules and habits are important, and can even be essential, but ultimately they can only do so much. Apart from God and his strength, we're helpless against the lies and temptations that will attempt to drive us away from him and from his word. That's why prayer is of the utmost importance here. God is stronger than the temptations that attack us, and he's infinitely greater than our faltering willpower. Go to him again and again, asking for strength to seek him day by day.

FINDING TIME

At this point you might be thinking, *Yes, I would love to study my Bible more. But I just don't have the time.*

First, you're not alone! This is a struggle for all of us. As teens, we're often overwhelmed with school, work, and other responsibilities. We wonder how we could possibly fit in anything extra. Maybe you barely have time to read a few verses every day, let alone seriously study it.

But again, it comes down to our priorities. Remember Mary and Martha? When Jesus came to the village of Bethany, he visited these two women and their brother Lazarus. Martha was busy, spending her time and effort serving Jesus—which was a good thing. But who was commended? It was her sister Mary, the one who spent her time sitting at Jesus's feet and listening to him (Luke 10:38–42).

Bible study is never a waste of time. Obviously there are responsibilities—such as school and work and family—that we can't just shove aside. But our relationship with God is the most important aspect of our lives. Sitting at the feet of Jesus is vital for our joy and our sanctification. And just like we make time for other things that are important to us (whether that's family, books, movies, hobbies, or hanging out with friends), we'll usually find we can make time for Bible study if it's truly a priority.

What takes up most of your free time? Where do you turn when you finish school or work or finally have time to be alone? For me it's usually books, social media, or some other form of entertainment. These things are certainly not bad. But what if making time for Bible study means we need to cut back on the time we spend with them? Are we willing to give up good things for the sake of the best thing? Perhaps it means taking on the challenge of getting up early. Are we willing to set our alarms thirty minutes earlier for the sake of God's word?

WHEN YOU DON'T FEEL LIKE IT

During my first few years in the Bible Bee, the competition was the only real reason I studied my Bible. Sure, I knew it was important—but I didn't care that much. It was all for the sake of winning. When I started to realize that about myself, I was frightened. Had all the time I spent studying and memorizing and reviewing been pointless? Had I done all of that for nothing?

Our motivation for studying God's word ought to be knowing him and enjoying his presence more and more. But sometimes it isn't. Sometimes we just don't want to spend time with him. Sometimes we're mired in guilt over a sin struggle that feels hopeless. Sometimes we're just apathetic, or we approach it from selfish, proud motives.

Does that mean we shouldn't study the Bible during those times? If we spend thirty minutes in Bible study that's motivated only by pride or a sense of duty, were those thirty minutes wasted?

The truth is, none of our obedience is perfect. Our Bible study, like everything else in our Christian life, will always be flawed by our own sin. But that doesn't mean it's useless. We serve a God who is so much bigger than our twisted motives, our apathy, and our sin. He is a God who "is able to do far more abundantly than all that we ask or think" (Eph. 3:20).

Paul learned more about the Old Testament than we can imagine while he was a proud Pharisee far from God. Once he was saved, he used that knowledge of the Old Testament to lead other Jews to Christ. His letters to the churches are filled with Old Testament quotations that explain and apply the gospel.

God's word is alive and powerful, and he is using it in our lives even when we don't realize it. He used the Scripture I learned out of pride and selfish ambition to give me a greater love for him. He will use even the Scripture you study in pride, apathy, or guilt to make you more like himself. We don't always feel like we're learning and growing through our study. In fact, we might feel like giving up. But the time we spend in God's word is never, ever wasted.

WHEN YOU JUST CAN'T

There will probably be times in your life where you just aren't able to study the Bible. Maybe it's a family situation that fills every waking moment. Maybe it's an illness that makes it impossible to focus. Maybe it's simply a season of your life that's full of necessary responsibilities.

Know that in these situations, God does not fault you for not being able to spend time in his word. He put you here for a reason. As Jen Wilkin writes, "Give the Lord what you can and trust that he will honor your faithfulness in the small things. Trust that the Lord knows your circumstances better than you do and that he sees your desire to learn and grow."[1]

Cling to him—snatch at whatever time you have to read a few verses, to pray, or even to meditate on verses you already know when you're doing the dishes or standing in line at the grocery store. But don't be discouraged that you aren't able to study your Bible right now. He will bring you through this as well, and maybe your study will be all the sweeter when you're finally able to return to it.

These situations are also another good reason to immerse ourselves in God's word while we do have the time and ability. If we have his word "[treasured] in our heart" (Ps. 119:11), then we'll have something we can cling to in the hard days or seasons.

AVOIDING DISTRACTIONS

How many times have you sat down to read your Bible—and been distracted? It might be the phone, a sibling, or a parent with a question. Suddenly, you find you only have a few minutes left to study.

We've all been there. Sometimes distractions are unavoidable—if your mom asks you to go do your chores, you'd better go do them! But we don't need to make it harder for ourselves. There are plenty of steps we can take to avoid or eliminate distractions when we're trying to study the Bible.

When it comes to distraction, devices are often the biggest offenders. Can you put your phone (or tablet, or computer) on silent or turn it all the way off so the notifications won't interrupt you? How about leaving it in another room so you won't be tempted to look at it?

Other people in the house can also be distracting. Of course, siblings and parents are more than distractions—they're family. God has given them to us as the friends, allies, and mentors who will hopefully stay by our side the rest of our life. Granted, sometimes that's hard to see (and sometimes, sadly, families are broken and don't reflect God's design). But if our zeal to study the Bible leads us to be unkind to our siblings or parents, we're missing something important. God's word ought to lead us to love our family more—not less.

That's why we should do our best to choose our study time wisely. Is there a time of day you know your family will be busy and likely need your help? Will somebody be loudly practicing an instrument? Is it the one part of the day when you can spend time with your siblings? That may not be the best time to schedule your Bible study.

Use your common sense. If the kitchen always has people running through it, don't do your study at the kitchen table. If the house is always loud, can you go outside? What about to your room? My favorite time to study is in the early morning, when my brothers aren't up yet, and the house is quiet.

Many of the distractions we face don't come from outside, however. They come from our own brain. Have you ever been reading the Bible when a phrase sets off a train of thoughts, and five minutes later you find yourself staring into space and not thinking about the text at all? Those are the distractions we have to fight the hardest. And we can't do it without God's help.

This, again, is why prayer is so important. We can only fight against distractions in our Father's strength. We'll discuss prayer more fully in the next chapter, but remember that when you're seeking to know God in his word, there will be opposition—from outside or from within your own heart. Only in God's power can we defeat it.

DON'T DISCOUNT BIBLE READING

While we're talking about daily routines, I don't want to discount the importance of simply reading your Bible. Although we can't stop there, it is important to our spiritual formation.

We already talked about the metanarrative of the Bible. It's one overarching story—the true story of how God redeemed his creation. And an important part of studying the Bible is becoming familiar with that big story.

When we study a book of the Bible, the first step is to get an overview by reading straight through it. In the same way, reading through the whole Bible helps us get an overview of the overall thrust of Scripture. When we read through the Bible, we see the metanarrative of history in all its glory. Then, as we dig deep into specific parts of it, we can better understand where they fit into the big story.

There isn't one right way or perfect plan for reading through the Bible. The way your friend or pastor does it may or may not be right for you. You can read it in a year, or two years, or ninety days. You can read straight through, or chronologically, or the Old and New Testaments at the same time. You can stick to a plan, or take it at your own pace.

In his book *Habits of Grace*, David Mathis says, "Read for breadth, study for depth."[2] How you balance those two is up to you and depends on your own situation. You might be able to do both at once, or you might choose to intersperse seasons of reading broadly with seasons of studying deeply. For instance, if you're part of a study with your church or youth group (which provides depth), when the group takes a break, you could read several chapters a day during the time you normally devote to studying (which would provide some breadth).

Remember that Bible-reading plans and schedules exist to serve as tools—not to enslave you. They're helpful to keep you on track, but if you need to modify them to fit your own situation, you're always free to do that.

Make Bible reading and study a priority in your heart and life, and seek God in prayer for wisdom as you do. He promises to answer—and his living, active word is at work in your heart no matter which method, schedule, or plan you choose (Heb. 4:12).

STUDYING IN COMMUNITY

So far, we've mostly been discussing personal Bible study—studying on your own. But the truth is, some of the best Bible study is that which is shared.

God designed us for community. He made us to live out our lives in connection with others. Beginning in the garden of Eden, relationship and community have been essential to human existence.

In creating the church, God gave us an entirely new level of community. He made us part of his body (Eph. 1:22–23), living stones being built up together into his temple (1 Pet. 2:5). Now Christians from every cultural, social, and ethnic background are brothers and sisters.

Our culture today has exalted the individual. Independence is prized. But God made us dependent on one another as well as on him. In the New Testament, the church is described as a body, where every individual part is both necessary and dependent on all the others as we work together for a cause greater than any of us.

That's why studying the Bible in a group setting is so important. "Bible study certainly does happen at a personal level, but within community it takes on dimension and accountability that it would not otherwise have."[3] Bible study gives us accountability to accurately interpret the text, and it also provides grounds for deeper fellowship with one another.

PROTECTING THE TRUTH

In his very last epistle, Paul told Timothy, "Do your best to present yourself to God as one approved, a worker who has no need to be ashamed, rightly handling the word of truth" (2 Tim. 2:15).

We must accurately handle God's word. This is our Creator's own revelation to us! We can't take it lightly or use it however we want. We need to take care that we're observing, interpreting, and applying it correctly.

That's why we need community. If we come to the table with a self-centered view of a text, other people who have studied the same passage can call us out. If we're confused, they can come alongside to help. They can show us something in the text we may not have noticed, point out a cross-reference we missed, or bring up another interpretation that makes more sense. They can help us stay grounded in the word.

Our fellow studiers can even bring up applications we may not have noticed. Perhaps I focused my study on how the text revealed God's holiness, and my friend focused on how it reveals his love. Both of us can help each other grow in the knowledge of God through what we've learned. Perhaps I focused on how the command to love others applies to my relationship with my family, and my brother or sister noticed how it applies to a pressing social issue. Both of us can learn from one another.

God works through his body to grow us individually. I need what the Holy Spirit is teaching my friends through his word as much as they need what he's teaching me in my personal study.

STRENGTHENED FELLOWSHIP

In 1 John 1:3, the apostle John explained to his readers why he was writing: he was proclaiming the gospel—what he had seen and heard of Christ—so his readers could have fellowship with him. He couldn't have fellowship with people who didn't believe the true gospel.

David Mathis says this about fellowship: "It is a 'partnership in the gospel' (Phil. 1:5) among those giving their everything to 'advance the gospel' (1:12), knit together for 'progress and joy in the faith' (1:25)."[4]

True fellowship happens around the gospel, between Christians who love God and are passionate about knowing him more.

Too often, our relationships in the church don't go beyond conversation about our own lives or our favorite movies. Those conversations are great, and they're an important part of getting to know each other, but if we want true Christian fellowship, we can't stop there. We should center our friendships around what really matters: God himself.

Some of my very best friendships were formed through the National Bible Bee Competition, even with people who were competing against me. The reason is that the prize wasn't the focus of the competition. Yes, the competition was fun, and it wasn't as if we didn't want to win. But that wasn't the ultimate goal. The goal was knowing and loving God more, and as we studied God's word together, we drew closer not only to God, but to each other. Interestingly, I didn't start forming these friendships until I began to experience the power of God's word in my own life. As my own goals shifted from winning a competition to seeking to know God better, my relationships with other believers grew.

Friendships happen around something we have in common. They might happen between people who love the same sports team, or have the same hobby, or even support the same good cause. "Friendship," C. S. Lewis wrote, "is born at the moment when one man says to another 'What! You too? I thought that no one but myself . . .'"[5]

As Christian teenagers, we also have something in common— and it's the biggest thing in the world. We have been saved, ransomed, and redeemed by God himself. We are brothers and sisters in the body of Christ. We should all have the same goal: to know our God and pursue a deeper relationship with him. That's something that binds people together beyond any barriers our society could invent.

And studying God's word in community is one of the best ways to pursue him together. Studying the Bible as a group can strengthen your relationships with other Christians. It provides a platform to have serious conversations about God and the Bible and our Christian walk—conversations that often don't happen in those twenty minutes of fellowship time on Sunday mornings. It grounds our fellowship in something bigger than ourselves.

As self-focused as we are, this can require a big step out of our comfort zone. Maybe your youth group doesn't have any

Bible study groups. But could you join a study for men and/or women? We need friends who are both older and younger than we are, along with those our own age! Or what about starting a study with a few friends? That can seem intimidating, but if God leads you to do it, there are lots of resources to help you. Pray for wisdom and trust in God's leading; he will guide you to just the right place.

Seek out other Christians in your Bible study. As you do the hard thing of studying a passage in community, you'll learn together. You'll grow in Christ together. You'll strengthen and encourage one another as you discover more about our God.

QUESTIONS

1. What is the best place and time for you to study your Bible every day? Will you have to make any changes to your schedule?

2. Write down the distractions that most often keep you from Bible reading and study. What can you do to avoid or defeat them?

3. What opportunities do you have to study the Bible with others? How are you taking advantage of those opportunities?

GETTING STARTED
WITH BIBLE STUDY

I know I should get up early in the mornings. I really do. I know it when I hit the snooze button the first time, and when I hit it the fourth time. I know I have classes to work on, writing to get done, relationships to build, and a to-do list to cross off.

But despite that knowledge, I stay in bed. I think about how I need to get up and get going, but I'm too comfortable where I am to do anything just yet.

We've been talking a lot about studying the Bible. *Knowing* we ought to do it is one thing; actually *doing it* is a whole different story. At first, the very idea of studying the Bible for yourself can seem overwhelming. Where do you even start?

This is where the inductive study method comes in handy.

The inductive study method is basically the same way pastors and Bible teachers study their Bibles. It isn't some complicated system or crazy series of steps you have to do in perfect order. It's simply the process of coming to God's word and discovering what it says for yourself.

If you were researching ancient Greece, your best option would be to go to primary sources—ancient documents and artifacts—to learn about it. You would try to find out what the ancient Greeks themselves had to say. So in Bible study, we should go *first* to the Bible to see what it says.

Inductive Bible study takes you directly to God's word to discover him. It makes the Bible the first authority. With inductive study we go first to what God has said—not what someone else says about it, not what fits our preferences, and not what we want to hear. We let God teach us through his word.

THE THREE PILLARS OF INDUCTIVE STUDY

There are three pillars to the inductive study method: observation, interpretation, and application.

- Observation asks, "What does this passage say?"
- Interpretation asks, "What does this passage mean?"
- Application asks, "How does this truth change me?"

Over the next few chapters, we'll be looking more closely at each of these pillars. They're all essential to the process. If you don't know what the passage says, how can you understand what it means? And if you don't understand the meaning, how can you apply it correctly?

This process can go against our natural inclination when we come to the Bible. A lot of times we want to jump right to application. "How does this apply to me? What can I get out of it?" Have you noticed this in your own life? We want something to help us, encourage us, or tell us what to do *right now*.

There are two problems with this "apply to me now" approach. The first problem is that it makes the Bible about us. When we're just reading it to see what we can get out of it, we forget that the Bible is all about God. The point is his glory.

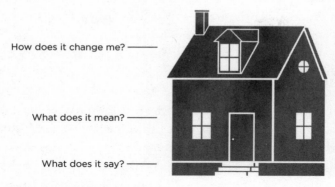

How does it change me? ——

What does it mean? ——

What does it say? ——

Illustration 7.1: Inductive Study

The other problem with going right to application is that if we jump to "How does this apply to me?" without first asking, "What does it say?" and "What does it mean?" we risk applying it wrongly. Bible study is like a building: knowing what the passage says is the foundation; knowing what it means is the wall built on that foundation. Application is the roof that rests on those walls. If you don't know what the passage means, how can you know how it applies to you?

That's why we always need all three steps of the inductive method: observation, interpretation, and application.

This may seem complicated already, but it's actually a process we use every day. Imagine you're installing a new lamp for your bedroom, and you have to use the instruction manual (pretend it's too complicated to just figure out on your own). The first thing you'd do is read it and see what it *says*. But if you're like me, some of the terms may not mean much to you! So you would look them up to see what the instruction manual is talking about—to understand what it *means*. Then you would *apply* this knowledge by following the instructions to install the lamp.

This is exactly what we do with inductive Bible study. First we discover what it says, then we work to understand what it means, and along the way—as we grow in our knowledge and understanding—we apply it to our lives.

One thing I want to point out here is that these three steps aren't completely separate. They're interwoven, building on each other and working together as you study. As you're using the tools of observation to discover what the text says, the meaning of a passage might become clear. Application might come as a result of interpretation, but it might also jump out at you during the stage of observation. The Holy Spirit is not boxed in by our methods. He works on his own terms, and he will use his word to change us.

THE TOOLBOX

The inductive study method gives us a lot of tools we can use to observe, interpret, and apply Scripture. That's what you're going to find in the next few chapters.

All these tools can be a bit overwhelming at first. It can feel like you've failed if you're not doing everything in every chapter in precisely the right order. But that's not how Bible study works. It's not about doing everything perfectly.

Think of the coming chapters as a toolbox. I'm not a great fixer-upper, but my dad and my brothers are, so our garage is filled with tools. We have shelves and boxes and drawers full of tools. We have tiny little wrenches and massive saws, hammers and levels and strange objects I don't even recognize. When my dad and brothers go to work on a project, they don't take out all those tools and use every single one. They pick and choose the tools that work best for the job at hand.

In the next few chapters, you'll discover many different tools. Some are essential—just as you would never start a fixer-upper project without a measuring tape, you should never study the Bible without them. Some are important, and you'll use them frequently, like the hammers and screwdrivers that get used all the time. Some are helpful, but you won't always need them—just like the table saw or the ⅝-inch wrench.

The goal of these chapters isn't to burden you with a long list of steps and directions. It's meant to equip you, to give you the variety of tools you need to understand God's word. As you become more comfortable with Bible study, you'll discover what works and what doesn't. Using the tools of inductive study will become more natural for you. Don't be discouraged if you don't use every one the first time.

BEGIN WITH PRAYER

Before we go any further, we need to stop. It's tempting to dive right into our study and start working—but we can't do this on our own. Before we study, we have to stop and seek God's help. Between our pride and our inadequacy, we desperately need him.

The Beast Named Pride

It's so easy to make Bible study about us. I know this from painful experience, and maybe you do too. We all have a beast in our hearts named Pride, and it loves to corrupt and hijack even the best things.

Oh, look! I'm studying the Bible. I know so much about it now. I definitely know more than she does. I'm so much more serious about my spiritual walk than he is.

We turn Bible study into one more area to prove our superiority and make us feel good about ourselves.

"Let us know; let us press on to know the LORD" (Hos. 6:3). That should be the heart of Bible study and our Christian walk. But knowledge *about* God can't be divorced from our relationship *with* God. Knowing our Savior is supposed to lead us to wonder and worship, which in turn leads to the desire to know him more. We're not just here to store up facts and clever phrases about our God. We have to come to God's word with a desire for *him*.

Our Own Inadequacy

In addition, if all we had for studying the Bible was our own intellect, we would be in big trouble. "The heart is deceitful above all things" (Jer. 17:9). On our own, we're liable to misinterpret the Scriptures, twist them to fit our own desires, and misuse them to build up our own self-righteousness while tearing others down.

We're handling weighty, everlasting things with fingers of dust. Why would we think our hands could hold these truths on our own? Why would we think our minds could comprehend the words of God himself unless he graciously gives us help? Why should we expect our hearts to be changed apart from his power?

RELIANCE ON HIS GRACE

Apart from God, we'll fail. We might learn a lot. We might even understand the intricacies of the most difficult verses. But if we're working from pride and a sense of self-sufficiency, all we'll do is understand it. It'll just be an intellectual exercise, no different from studying history or algebra.

Rather than relying on our own intelligence and hard work, we need to rely on God. Don't come to God's word with an attitude of, "I'm going to figure it out." Come to his word and ask him to teach you. Only he can truly open up the Scriptures to us so that we'll understand and stand in awe of the truth we behold. Only he can use his word to change us.

And the glorious news is that he not only *can* help us, but he *will*. We find numerous promises in the Bible that can give us great courage as we seek to know God through his word. First John 5:14–15 says, "And this is the confidence that we have toward him, that if we ask anything according to his will he hears us. And if we know that he hears us in whatever we ask, we know that we have the requests that we have asked of him." Whatever we ask, if it's according to God's will, he will hear, and he will answer. And if there's anything we can be sure is his will, it's that he wants us to know and love him more! So we can come before him with confidence to ask his help in knowing, understanding, and applying his word and be certain that he will answer.

Jen Wilkin writes, "Prayer is the means by which we implore the Holy Spirit to take up residence in our study time."[1] We need the Holy Spirit's assistance as we study. So before you begin studying, *pray*. Praise God for giving us his word. Confess to him that you can't understand or apply it on your own. Pray for wisdom as you decide what to study. Pray for perseverance and faithfulness, that what you start in joy won't fall by the wayside as you lose the initial excitement. Pray for focus, that you won't get distracted. Pray that God would show you more of himself and give you joy in him.

As you study, *pray*. Praise him for his attributes as you see him in his word. Confess sin as you're convicted by it. Pray for help in understanding. Pray that as you observe and interpret the Bible, God would use it to change you. Pray for strength to keep going and stand firm against spiritual attack.

After you study, *pray*. Praise God for who he is and what you learned. Confess sin that he brought to your attention. Pray that you would not forget, but the truth you've learned would imprint itself on your heart and mind and change the way you think, speak, and act. Pray for opportunities to share this truth with others.

It's possible to know a lot about God and be just as far from him as before. Apart from prayer and the work of the Holy Spirit, Bible study will never be more than an intellectual exercise. So be fervent and committed in asking God for help—because he promises to give it.

WHERE DO I START?

The first step is to decide what you'll actually be studying. Of course, all of the Bible is inspired by God, and all of it is useful and relevant to us today. However, if you're just getting started with serious Bible study, it might be best to start with a shorter epistle such as Colossians, Philippians, 2 Timothy, James, 1 Peter, or Ephesians. These books are packed full of doctrine and long enough to present a challenge without being so long that you'll get burned out.

Longer books such as Deuteronomy and Revelation also reward diligent study, but if you've never studied inductively before, it might be best to defer them for later. Once you've gained experience with Bible study, you can come back to these books and dive into the rich treasures they contain.

On a side note, you might be wondering why you should study an entire book. Why not do a shorter passage, or even a topical study? It's true that both of these approaches can have their place. However, we were meant to engage with books of the Bible in their entirety. Just as with any other book, each book of the Bible is a unit of thought and meaning, building a story or argument verse by verse, each part dependent on what comes before it. When you study an entire book, you can see the flow of the author's thought. You're much less likely to take things out of context, and it'll help you understand the original meaning of the text.

The other reason to study whole books is that it helps prevent us from picking and choosing the parts of the Bible we like. We need *all* of the Bible. We need to understand every aspect of God's character and every part of the story—even the parts we don't like very much. When we go straight through a book, from start to finish, it'll help defeat our natural tendency to avoid the parts that are hard to understand or that make us uncomfortable.

Again, seek God's help here. He knows exactly what you need to study right now, so ask him. If you're studying with someone else, get their input and see what they want to study. If you're part of a group, you may not even need to worry about choosing a book!

Don't stress over it, either. Again, every part of Scripture is part of God's communication to us: whether you study Colossians or 1 Chronicles, God can use it in your heart. The first book of the Bible I studied all the way through by myself was Nahum. Looking back, I probably wouldn't have picked that one—it was confusing in many places, and it didn't have the same comforting truths and promises that you might find in the epistles or the Psalms. But as I studied this difficult book, I got to see God's power, holiness, and justice on display in a way I never had before. It helped give me a better understanding of God's character.

Whatever you choose, do it in prayer and reliance on God. Then dive in and start studying in faith that God will use it in your life. You might be surprised at what he does.

WHAT YOU'LL NEED

You'll need a few materials for inductive Bible study. Don't worry, though! You should be able to find most of them around your home.

It goes without saying that you need a Bible for Bible study. However, you may not want to use your actual Bible for some of it, since you'll want to make markings in the text as you go along. The same goes for Bible apps: while helpful, they're usually harder to use for this kind of study.

If you don't like to mark in your Bible, you can print out the passage. There's no right or wrong way to do this. The way I do it is to copy and paste the entire book from an online Bible or Bible software, reformat it so each verse is on a separate line, and make sure the whole document is double spaced with wide margins. This leaves plenty of room for me to mark key words, write notes, and make lists.

How?

1 - In you, O Lord do I take refuge; let me never be put to shame!

2 - In your righteousness deliver me and rescue me; incline your ear to me, and save me!

3 - Be to me a rock of refuge, to which I may continually come; you have given the command to save me, for you are my rock and my fortress.

4 - Rescue me, O my God, from the hand of the wicked, from the grasp of the unjust and cruel man. *He asks God for deliverance because he trusts in him.*

5 - For you, O Lord, are my hope, my trust, O Lord, from my youth.

6 - Upon you I have leaned from before my birth; you are he who took me from my mother's womb. My praise is continually of you.

7 - I have been as a portent to many, but you are my strong refuge.

8 - My mouth is filled with your praise, and with your glory all the day.

9 - Do not cast me off in the time of old age; forsake me not when my strength is spent. *Does this mean he's old here?*

10 - For my enemies speak concerning me; those who watch for my life consult together *His enemies say God has forsaken him — he's asking God to prove them wrong.*

11 - and say, "God has forsaken him; pursue and seize him, for there is none to deliver him."

12 - O God, be not far from me; O my God, make haste to help me!

13 - May my accusers be put to shame and consumed; with scorn and disgrace may they be covered who seek my hurt.

14 - But I will hope continually and will praise you yet more and more.

Illustration 7.2: Formatted Bible Passage and Notes Example—Psalm 71[2]

Something else you'll find indispensable is a notebook. It doesn't have to be expensive—just somewhere to write things down. I use my notebook not just for writing notes and making lists, but also to jot down reflections on the passage; it becomes a sort of journal for what I'm learning as I study.

Writing utensils are also important. With these, you can go as plain or as fancy as you want. My essentials are a pencil, a pen, and a set of colored pencils. I use the colored pencils for marking key words (we'll talk more about that in a couple chapters). If you like to go all out with colors and styles, then you might want to get some highlighters or Flair pens (but you certainly don't have to).

When you get into interpretation, you'll want some tools to study Greek or Hebrew words and cross-references. There are books available for the purpose; the ones we'll discuss here are *Strong's Concordance* and the *Treasury of Scripture Knowledge*. Both of these can be found online for free.

Lastly, once you've studied the passage for yourself, you might find it helpful to read a commentary or listen to some sermons. I've included a list of good commentaries and sermon websites in Appendix A, although you may have some laying around your house as well. If you're not sure where to find good resources, ask your parents or pastor for suggestions.

EMBRACE THE PROCESS

As you begin studying, remember: Bible study is a skill. And like any other skill, it takes time to learn.

Chances are, you won't feel very confident the first time. You may not pick up everything that an experienced Bible student would or have the same breadth of biblical knowledge. And that's okay—you're *learning*. The important thing is that you're growing in your understanding of his word, little by little.

Your study may not always give you an application or specific encouragement right in the moment. It may feel boring. You might not see any results. Will you trust that God is still growing you? He is still using his word to bring you to a deeper knowledge of himself. Jen Wilkin writes that "gaining Bible literacy requires allowing our study to have a cumulative effect—across weeks, months, years—so that the interrelation of one part of Scripture to another reveals itself slowly and gracefully, like a dust cloth slipping inch by inch from the face of a masterpiece."[3]

QUESTIONS

1. Have you ever studied the Bible inductively before? If so, what was the best part of the experience? If not, what about it is exciting or intimidating to you?

2. Why do you think it's important to have all three pillars—observation, interpretation, and application? Do you normally approach the Bible this way?

3. Write out a prayer as you begin your study.

8

THE MOST IMPORTANT TOOL

I sat around the table with a few other teenage girls, Bibles open. The passage in front of us was one of my favorites. It happened to be one I'd been studying on my own, and I was glad we got to discuss it together.

But, as the leader started talking about a particular verse, I frowned. Something didn't sound quite right. I glanced around in confusion to see if anyone else reacted, as what she said seemed an increasingly bizarre interpretation. *Wait . . . what?*

Have you ever been there? Listening to a message or reading a book, when suddenly something doesn't sound quite right? A little alarm in the back of your head starts to go off as you wonder whether that *really* fits with what the rest of the Bible says.

Misinterpretation of the Bible is sadly common—even among well-meaning teachers and students. Often, with the best of intentions, we use a verse of Scripture to support our message, even though that verse may not mean what we think it means. How can we know if a teacher or author is accurately interpreting a text? And just as importantly, how can we make sure *we* don't come up with some erroneous interpretation to mislead ourselves and others?

There are lots of tools we can use to make sure we correctly observe and interpret the Bible, and we'll look at several of them in the next few chapters. However, the first place we should always look is *context*.

WHAT IS CONTEXT?

Context is, quite literally, "what goes with the text." It's the verses and chapters that surround the passage you're studying. It can also have to do with the history and culture that informed the writing of the passage.

This term isn't unique to Bible study. You're probably familiar with it from everyday life. If you're with two friends who don't know each other, and you reference an inside joke you have with one of them, the other won't understand. Why? Because they don't know the *context*. They weren't there when the joke originated. They don't have the relationship with that person that you do.

We can't approach our study without looking at the context. Would you open up a book, read one paragraph from somewhere in the middle, and try to understand it? Of course not! The paragraph wouldn't make any sense. Yet that's often what we try to do with the Bible. We attempt to interpret verses, paragraphs, and chapters on their own, apart from the larger context of the text around them and the rest of the Bible.

We cannot properly understand a verse or passage of the Bible without its context. If we try, we run the risk of grossly misinterpreting Scripture.

AN EXAMPLE FROM ROMANS

Romans 8:28 says, "And we know that God causes all things to work together for good to those who love God, to those who are called according to his purpose."

This is a beautiful, powerful promise from God. But it's easy to take the wrong way. When we only look at this one verse, we can get the wrong impression. It can seem like the "good" Paul is talking about is something immediate—like whatever hard thing you're going through is going to bring you greater prosperity, or better friendships, or renewed health.

That may be the case. God is a merciful Father, and sometimes he works this way. But Hallmark-style endings are not what this verse is talking about. Look at the rest of the passage:

> And we know that for those who love God all things work together for good, for those who are called according to his purpose. *For those whom he foreknew he also predestined to be conformed to the image of his Son, in order that he might be the firstborn among many brothers.* And those whom he predestined he also called, and those whom he called he also justified, and those whom he justified he also glorified. (Rom. 8:28–30)

We're called according to his purpose. And what is that purpose? *That we would be conformed to Christ's image.*

The truth is, while we're on this sin-cursed earth, still fighting the evil lingering within us, everything is not always going to work out for good in a way we can immediately see. Can years of chronic pain, or the deep hurt of losing a loved one, or the ache of depression truly be made "worth it" by something on this earth? What about Christians who live and die in horrendous conditions and never experience anything we would call "good"?

But being conformed and transformed into the image of our Savior is a good beyond anything in this world. It's something eternal that will never pass away. And ultimately, it will bring us far more joy than any material blessing.

That may sound like trite comfort, but it goes far deeper than saying things will be made right in this world alone. Our world is still subject to the effects of sin, and it will ultimately pass away. Rather than offer us temporary blessings here, God promises to make us like his own Son, transformed into the glorious image of God himself. That doesn't negate the pain—we still hurt. We still suffer. But we're offered a far greater blessing at the end of our trials here: being made "perfect and complete, lacking in nothing" (James 1:4).

Verses like Romans 8:28 are why we have to be very careful not to take things out of context. It may sound good—we would all love some assurance that whatever we're going through is going to result in better circumstances down the road. But if we cling to that hope, we may be disillusioned in the end. Far better to cling to the true hope that this passage—and the rest of the Bible—offers.

BIBLICAL CONTEXT

If context is so important to our understanding of the Bible, we need to incorporate it into our study. How we do that is going to depend on what we're studying and what kind of context we're talking about.

There are three different types of context: biblical, historical, and cultural.

Biblical context is probably the simplest of the three—but at the same time it's the most important. Remember how the inductive method makes the Bible the primary authority in our study? We always want to let Scripture interpret Scripture. This starts with context.

Biblical context is the text that surrounds and explains the verse or passage you're studying. It might simply be the rest of the paragraph, as in our Romans 8:28 passage above. Expanding outward, it's the rest of the chapter and even the rest of the book. Ultimately, the entire biblical story contributes to our understanding of every verse within it.

If you're studying one verse or short passage, it's essential that you know the contents of at least the verses immediately surrounding it, and preferably the rest of the chapter. This will prevent you from making any hasty judgments.

For example, as a student, one of the verses I've most often seen quoted to my age group is Jeremiah 29:11:

> For I know the plans I have for you, declares the LORD, plans
> for welfare and not for evil, to give you a future and a hope.

That sounds wonderful! Taken by itself, it seems like God is promising us bright, successful futures without any troubles. But then, what about all the times it doesn't go like that? What about those who haven't gotten the jobs they wanted, or seem stuck with no place to go, or have all their plans overturned by a chronic illness or a major disaster? Does Jeremiah 29:11 still apply?

The problem is, we never read Jeremiah 29:1–10. It's actually a letter—from the prophet Jeremiah to the people of Israel who were exiled in Babylon. He's telling them to live and raise their families in Babylon, and after seventy years God will restore them to their land. Jeremiah 29:11 was actually written as a proclamation of hope to God's chosen nation living in exile. The reason it doesn't seem to work in our lives is that it wasn't spoken to us in the first place.

Does that mean we can't learn from this verse? Of course not. Again, *all* Scripture is given to us by God. In this passage we see attributes of God that can give us hope and peace. We see that he is faithful to his covenant people. We see that he is merciful, gracious, and compassionate, and that he *never* goes back on his promises. There are legitimate and wonderful applications to be made from this verse. Reading it in context will help us be careful not to misunderstand it.

Where possible, it's also important to be familiar with the rest of the book. Most books of the Bible have a definite structure and progression of thought, and we can't fully understand one part without the others. For instance, the various exhortations in the last three chapters of Ephesians are excellent instructions that we need to follow—but they have to be understood in light of the first three chapters, which are a glorious explanation of the gospel. Paul's point isn't just to give us more rules to live by, but to help us embrace the gospel and show us how holy living will flow out from it. If we only looked at certain verses in Ephesians, we might get the idea that Paul just wants us to work harder at obedience. But when we see those verses in the context of the whole book, we understand how obedience flows from an understanding of the grace God has shown us in the gospel.

Again, this is why it's so important that we study books of the Bible rather than picking and choosing the chapters and verses we like. When you're studying an entire book, you'll be familiar with the overall structure and with the contents of each chapter. That way, when you go deep with a specific passage, you'll already have that context in mind.

Ultimately, the entire Bible is context. The Bible is one over-arching story, and you can't understand one part of it without looking at how that part fits into the big picture.

Of course, you can't read through the entire Bible every time you want to understand a specific verse. Familiarity with the whole story takes time. But as you make a habit of studying God's word, digging deep, and discovering his truth for yourself, you'll grow in your understanding of Scripture as a whole.

Remember that it's a process. It'll take a good deal of patience and study. But over time, it will pay off. As you grow in your knowledge and understanding, you'll start to see the connections. What you learned from one book will help you interpret another. You'll be listening to a message or reading another part of the Bible and start connecting the dots to what you've already studied. As you keep studying the Bible, you'll see more and more clearly how the different parts of it relate and help explain each other.

HISTORICAL CONTEXT

The Bible was written by real people who had real things happening around them. They were part of the same history you learn about in World History class—Moses walked among the temples and obelisks of ancient Egypt, and Paul's sandals slapped against the famous roads of the Roman Empire.

Often, this history is important in understanding what they wrote. No one could understand a biography of Abraham Lincoln without knowing a little about the American Civil War. In the same way, we often won't fully understand the Bible if we don't know anything about the events and historical figures that surround it.

A good example of the need for historical context is Jesus's words in Luke 21:6, where he told the people admiring the Jewish temple, "As for these things that you see, the days will come when there will not be left one stone upon another that will not be thrown down." This was shocking and confusing to his listeners at the time. How could Jesus say such a thing about the magnificent temple itself? However, today we know that exact thing happened in AD 70 when the Jewish temple was destroyed by the Romans.

Another example is Peter's admonition to "be subject for the Lord's sake to every human institution, whether it be to the emperor as supreme, or to governors as sent by him to punish those who do evil and to praise those who do good" (1 Pet. 2:13–14). Although everyone chafes against governmental authority sometimes (who likes all those regulations?), this exhortation takes on a whole new meaning when we realize that Peter's epistle was written during the reign of the Roman emperor Nero. Rome could already be a harsh master, but Nero would soon begin a spectacularly cruel persecution of Christians. Despite this, Peter told his readers that, for God's sake, they should submit to the government over them.

So, how do we discover historical context? It can seem a bit daunting, but don't worry—you don't have to take a history class for it!

The first thing to do is to see what you can discover from the text itself. You'll probably want to do this during your overview (which we'll talk about in the next chapter). Does the text give you any clues about when it was written or when the events took place? If it says, "During the eighth year of King So-and-So," that's a great place to start. A lot of Old Testament books will give you this kind of information, but you can sometimes find it in the New Testament too (Luke 2, for instance).

Look for other clues as well. Are any historical figures mentioned? Any places or events? Mark those and write them down. Act like a detective—see what you can figure out based on what you find.

The next step is to see what help archaeologists and historians can offer. This is where a Bible dictionary or the introduction to a commentary will come in handy. Historians know a lot, for instance, about the history of Babylon or ancient Rome, and a good Bible dictionary or commentary will include lots of basic information. In a Bible dictionary, find the name of the book you're studying and there ought to be information about when it was written and what was happening in the world at the time. If you have a good commentary, it should include something about the historical context in the introduction to the book. Just make sure you only read the introduction! You can get back to commentaries, but only after you've studied the book for yourself.

CULTURAL CONTEXT

Cultural context is very similar to historical context in that it deals with the circumstances surrounding the writing of the book.

However, instead of historical events, it deals with the culture of the author, the recipients, or the people included in the narrative. While historical and cultural context are similar, they deal with different aspects of a time period.

For instance, if someone five hundred years from now was going to study the *historical* context of America from 2000–2020, they would look at historical figures (e.g., George W. Bush, Barack Obama, and Donald Trump) and events (e.g., the World Trade Center attack on 9/11 and the invention of Google). If they wanted to study the *cultural* context, they would look at factors such as the rise of the Internet, social media, the emphasis on social justice, consumer culture, and Americans' obsession with appearance.

If you were going to a different country, you would probably encounter a different culture. People might do certain things differently, or they might have different ways of speaking or thinking. You wouldn't want to assume they do everything the way you're used to. You would learn about and respect their culture.

It's the same way with the Bible. If possible, we should do our best to understand the customs of the people we're reading about, the way they thought, and how their culture worked—especially since it's often very different from our own culture. Things that would have made perfect sense to the readers at the time might not make sense to us.

The narrative about the Samaritan woman Jesus met at the well is a good example for the importance of understanding cultural context (John 4:1–26). It may not seem that odd to us that she would be there by herself in the middle of the day. But in ancient Middle Eastern culture, women didn't go to the well at noon. They went in the morning and evening, when it was cool outside, and generally there would be a large group of women chatting and gossiping together. For this woman to be by herself marks her as a social outcast even among her own people (who were already considered outcasts by the Jews).

Further, women were often degraded or considered "less-thans" in ancient times. For a respected teacher to stop and talk to any woman—not to mention an outcast Samaritan—would have been shocking or even scandalous. Yet not only did Jesus stop and speak to her for a while, he graciously offered her the good news of eternal life. He then made her the witness who would bring that same good news to her entire city. When we understand the cultural context of this narrative, we can better comprehend the vast grace and mercy of Jesus Christ.

So, how do we learn about cultural context? When we're talking about ancient Israel, we can learn a lot just by looking at other parts of the Bible. When the Gospels talk about the Passover, we can look back at Exodus and other books in the Old Testament to learn what the Passover was and how Israel had celebrated (or failed to celebrate) it throughout their history. Again, if we were studying Ruth, we would need to go back to laws in Exodus and Leviticus to understand why Ruth was gleaning in a field and why it was so important for Boaz to marry her.

Just as with historical context, Bible dictionaries are helpful too. For instance, we can learn a lot from ancient Jewish sources about the Pharisees and their role in Jewish culture. Knowing how respected they were, and the exalted place they occupied in society, can help us understand just how shocking it was for Jesus to openly call them out for their hypocrisy.

All of this can seem pretty overwhelming, especially at first. Again, don't feel like you have to do everything the first time. With practice, you'll learn how and when to discover the historical and cultural context of the passage you're studying. This is also another way studying in a group is helpful. Others in the group might research something you wouldn't even have thought about looking up. You can learn from their study, and they can learn from yours.

In the end, context is about realizing that no part of the Bible truly stands alone. It's all connected together, and it's also connected to the culture and events of the world in which the author was writing. We have to be willing to put in the time and work to read the rest of the chapter, to understand the flow of thought throughout the book, and to become familiar with the entirety of the biblical story. We have to be humble enough to step outside our preconceived notions into a history and culture that may be unfamiliar or even uncomfortable for us.

We need to look at Scripture as it was written—in the context of its own history, its own culture, and the rest of God's word.

QUESTIONS

For the next few chapters, this space is where you'll get a chance to practice the skills you're learning. We'll be going through the book of 3 John. It's a short book—perfect for practice—and full of truth. You can do these exercises as you finish reading each chapter or wait until you've finished this book.

1. Start by reading through the book of 3 John. It's only fifteen verses, so it shouldn't take long! This will help you get the context of the whole book. If you have extra time, try reading 1 and 2 John as well. This will give you the context of the rest of John's epistles.

2. Next, look for historical context. Did you notice any clues in the text?

3. Now go ahead and look up 3 John in a Bible dictionary, or read the introduction to 3 John in a commentary or study

Bible. What can you learn about the time and place of its writing? (If you need help finding a good dictionary, I recommend *Easton's Bible Dictionary*, available on Blue Letter Bible here: https://www.blueletterbible.org/search/Dictionary/viewTopic .cfm?topic=ET0002093.)

9

OBSERVATION:

"WHAT DOES IT SAY?"

When I was about eleven or twelve, one of my dearest wishes was to fly on a plane. I hadn't flown since I was little. The spacious, polished interior of the Tampa airport held a sense of mystery and adventure, and when we dropped off my dad so he could go on a business trip, I wanted him to take me along.

When I finally did get to ride on a plane, the takeoff was exhilarating. We lifted off the ground, and suddenly we were in the air. I stared out the window as the city got smaller and smaller down below.

I've been on airplanes many times since then. Flying has lost a bit of its appeal (cramped, crowded spaces really aren't my thing), but I still think the experience of taking off and landing has no rival. That's why I always grab the window seat—I'll spend the whole time staring at the ground and marveling at how tiny the cars look, the design of the streets, and the identical little houses.

We've talked about when and where to study the Bible, and we've laid a foundation of basic principles. Now we need to start studying. But we can't begin with walking down the streets of observation or diving into the messy weeds of interpretation. First, we need a thirty-thousand-foot view. That's where we'll start— using tools of observation to get an overview of the whole book before we descend for a closer look at chapters and verses.

Remember the toolbox we talked about? This chapter might be the most packed with tools.

Remember: these different methods and steps are here to serve your understanding of God's word. They're very helpful, sometimes necessary, but they're still just the tools. Don't get so caught up in following every step that you lose sight of the big picture. We're here to behold our God, not just check off a list of instructions.

With that in mind—and beginning everything with prayer— let's dive in.

SEE THE BIG PICTURE

Our first step is to get the "big picture" of the book we're studying. This is called an overview. Often I'll spend a week or more on overview, so I can understand the book's context and flow of thought. This step gives us a map so we can navigate the streets and forests of observation and interpretation without losing our way.

The best way to start is by reading. That may not feel very "study-ish," but it's essential. Reading through the book you're studying will help you see it as a whole. It'll let you examine the flow of thought and fit the chapters and verses into the overall structure of the book.

If you can, read through the whole book in one sitting. This may not work for a longer book, but if you're doing something like Ruth or 2 Timothy, it's very doable. How fast you read isn't really important here. If you can get through the whole thing in twenty minutes, great! I find it usually takes me longer, and that's all right too. If you have trouble staying focused for the entire book, listening to an audio Bible while you follow along in the text might help.

As you're reading, keep your eyes on the big picture. Don't get bogged down in every detail. You may not understand everything the author is saying, and you may have a lot of questions but—for now—don't stop to figure them out. Write them down on a separate piece of paper, if you're so inclined, and keep going.

Once you've read through the book once or twice, write down the main theme. What's the primary message? Sum it up in one sentence if you can. Don't feel like this has to be perfect—it should just be what shows up in a preliminary reading. You have all the freedom in the world to change it as you learn more through your study. We're still just trying to get the "big picture" of what this book is about so we have context to dig deep later.

If it's a "teaching book," like an epistle, see if you can find the author's main point—the message the rest of the book revolves around. If it's a narrative book, you might just summarize the events. For instance, "God frees his people from Egypt" would be a great place to start summarizing if you're studying Exodus.

Remember, you don't need to include all the details or even understand them all. That will come later.

BACKGROUND INFORMATION

The next thing to look for is the background:

- *Who* wrote this book?
- *What* circumstances surrounded its writing?
- *Where* was it written (and in some cases, *where* would it have been read)?
- Most importantly, *why* was it written?

Do some of these questions sound familiar? They should! These are all context questions, and we need to answer them if we can. Remember: start with what you can find in the text, then go to other sources.

Author and recipient: Knowing who wrote the book is obviously important. If it's a letter that starts with, "Paul, an apostle of Jesus Christ . . . to the church at such and such a place," then your job just got a lot easier! Still, find out what you can about these people. This is where colored pencils help. I like to mark each reference to the author in one color and each reference to the recipient in another. Then you can write down everything you observe about the main characters of the book. You might even want to devote a day of study to this author-and-recipient process.

If it's not a letter (or it doesn't say who wrote it), then it's dictionary time. See if you can find out what scholars have discovered about the author of your book as well as its intended audience.

Important places: Where was the book written? Where were its readers? Or, if it's a narrative, where did the events take place? This is especially helpful with Paul's epistles, since he traveled a lot and started churches in many different cities. It's even more vital when you're studying historical books, such as Old Testament narratives, that revolve around different places and the people who inhabited them.

Break out your detective skills again and see what you can learn about the city of Ephesus, Bethlehem, or the land of Moab. If your book deals with many different places, such as in a Gospel, then you might want to leave this step until you study the individual chapters. But if possible, try to get an overview of where the events took place. A map of ancient Israel and the surrounding area is helpful (many good ones can be found online, and often there are a few at the back of your Bible).

Historical context: You knew we would end up here, didn't you? This is the point where you get to use everything you've learned about discovering historical context and apply it to the book you're studying. What time period is this? Was the book written during the reign of one of the kings of Israel? And if so, what can you learn about that king? Or was it written by Paul— and at what point during his travels? Once you've written down what you observe from the text, use Bible dictionaries and cross-references to learn more.

Purpose: Finally, the most important thing you need to understand about any book at this stage is, "Why was it written?" Many times—especially with epistles—the book's purpose ties directly back to the theme. For instance, Jude wrote his short epistle "appealing to you to contend for the faith" (Jude 3). The theme of the book is contending for the faith against ungodly people who have snuck into the church.

John's Gospel was written "so that you may believe that Jesus is the Christ, the Son of God; and that believing you may have life in his name" (John 20:31). The Gospel of John tells the events of Jesus's ministry, and it's structured in such a way as to show that he was the Christ. Understanding why a book was written can give you a framework for understanding it. Again, the purpose of some books won't be clear at first glance, and sometimes you won't discover the purpose until you've done some work studying. But if you can find it at this stage, it will help guide the rest of your study.

ASK QUESTIONS

Now we're done with our airplane-window view. We're landing at the airport and starting to walk the streets. Like a detective or a journalist, we'll investigate at the chapter level and get all the facts before we start to interpret them.

What's the first thing that any good detective or reporter does? After they glance around and take in the scene, they immediately start asking questions. "What did you see? When did it happen? What was the suspect wearing?"

How?

That's what we have to do with Bible study. Once we get the big picture, we start asking questions about the text. There are six specific questions we should be asking: *Who? What? When? Where? Why? How?* These are our observation questions.

Here are some examples of questions we might ask about a text:

- *Who* wrote it? *To whom* was it written? *Who* are the main people (or beings) mentioned?
- *What* are the main events of the narrative? *What* are the main points the author is trying to get across? *What* is going on?
- *When* did these events happen? *When* are they going to happen? How much time passed between two events?
- *Where* did the events happen? *Where* were the author and recipients of the epistle?
- *Why* did something happen? *Why* is the author making this point?
- *How* did the Israelites defeat their enemy? *How* is God going to redeem his people? *How* was the church disobeying, and *how* does the author rebuke them?

It often helps to write down the answers to each of these questions in a notebook. Keep in mind that you're not trying to ask all these questions about every verse. Ask them about the chapter as a whole. You also may not find answers to each of these questions (many epistles never give information about location or time period, for example). Just discover what you can from the text, without trying to read anything into it.

When I started studying on my own, this aspect of inductive study was confusing and overwhelming. But it helped me to realize that it's actually a process we use every day.

Imagine if I showed you a news article with the title, "Massive Alligator Shocks Neighbors." As you started reading it, you would have a lot of questions in mind. "*What* kind of alligator? *How* did it shock the neighbors (just by being there, or did it eat someone's pet)? *How* big is 'massive' (is that according to someone from Michigan or someone from Florida)? *Who* were the neighbors? *Where* was it (and was it near my house)? *When* did this happen (last night, or last week)? *Why* was the 'gator there at all? *What* is going to be done about it?"

Any good news article will answer all those questions, because newspaper reporters know we instinctively want the answers to "Who, what, when, where, why, and how?"—especially when it's something that might affect us (like a huge alligator in the neighborhood!).

When you approach Scripture, keep all these same questions in mind. It may seem awkward or unwieldy at first, but as you keep asking them, it'll become more natural. Let them be in the back of your head throughout your study. Get into the habit of coming to Scripture not like a consumer waiting to be fed, but like a detective on a hunt for answers.

Here's an example of some questions you might ask and their answers for Psalm 71. If you're not familiar with the psalm, you might want to go ahead and read it first.

- *Who is writing the psalm?* We're not told, so we'll call him the psalmist. (This is an example of when you won't find the answer to a question in the text.)
- *Who is involved?* The psalmist, the Lord, and the wicked/ enemies.
- *What is going on?* The psalmist is praying for deliverance, his enemies are plotting against him, and the psalmist is praising God and trusting in him.
- *When are these things happening?* The only clue we have is in verses 9 and 18, where the psalmist prays that God will not forsake him when he is old. That might mean the psalmist is old in this chapter, although we can't be sure.

How?

- *Where are these things happening?* Again, the psalm doesn't give us an answer to this question.
- *Why is the psalmist praying for deliverance?* Because God is his rock, his fortress, and his hope (vv. 2–5).
- *Why does the psalmist ask God not to forsake him?* Because his enemies are saying that God has forsaken him (vv. 9–11).
- *How is God to deliver the psalmist?* In his righteousness (v. 2).
- *How does the psalmist hope?* Continually (v. 14).

The purpose of asking observation questions isn't just to check it off the list of things to do in Bible study. It's to slow down, focus in on the text, and really see what it's saying. It's easy to just read through it once or twice and think we've seen everything there. Asking questions can help us see things and make connections we wouldn't have see or made before. We need to dig deep and spend time with the text, and questions are one of the best ways to do that.

By the way, as you're going through the process of observation, you'll probably come up with some questions of interpretation: "What does this mean?" or "What's the connection between these two ideas?" When you come across these, write them down in your notebook or in the margin of your printed copy of the text for later. We'll get to them soon!

KEY WORDS AND LISTS

Now that we're starting to get a grasp on the passage through big-picture observation and asking questions, we're ready to dig a little deeper by examining the words that are key to the text. This is one of my favorite parts of observation. You can learn so much from studying key words and making lists! Who knew, right?

What Is a Key Word?

A *key word* is a word that is central to the meaning of the passage. It's a word that, if taken away, would leave the passage meaningless. Often it's repeated several times, although it may only be used once or twice.

For example, the biggest key word in the book of 1 John is "love." It's used over and over throughout the book, and it's central to the apostle's message. In Genesis 1, "created" and "made" are key words (obviously!). In Jude, "ungodly" is key because it's the primary way Jude describes the antagonists.

If you've ever taken a literature class, this may sound familiar. You've probably had a teacher write out a passage from a book or poem on a whiteboard and underline or circle the words that are important to understanding the author's meaning ("nevermore" in Edgar Allan Poe's "The Raven" is a good example). Remember, the Bible is more than a great piece of literature, but it's certainly not less. Many of the techniques of literary analysis you learn in a good literature class can be applied to Bible study.

MARKING KEY WORDS

Just as you might underline, circle, or draw squiggly lines around key words in literature class, you can do it with the Bible. Marking key words helps them stand out. It can also allow you to see their relationship to each other and to the text as a whole.

Key-word-marking methods are nearly as varied as the students who use them. You can simply underline with your pen or pencil, you can use highlighters or colored pencils to color-code the words, you can draw symbols, or you can combine all these ideas. Don't feel like you're required to use a specific system. Do whatever you need to help the key words stick out to you. (And this is why having the text printed out on a separate sheet of paper is nice, if you don't want to mark up your Bible too much.)

How do you decide what to mark? Start by looking for repeated words. (Words such as "the" or "and" don't count!) If a word such as "love," "righteousness," "world," or "works" is repeated several times, it's probably worth marking. Look for words that are central to the passage's message. Repetition often indicates importance, but sometimes a very important word is only used a couple of times.

As you mark key words, remember to mark synonyms (words that have the same or similar meaning) and pronouns. For instance, if I'm marking references to God, I would also mark "he," "his," or "you" if they refer to God. If I'm marking "deliverance" in a psalm, I would probably also mark "save" and "rescue."

References to Deity

Since God is at the center of the biblical story, references to him are *always* key words. You almost always want to mark these. (Narratives such as the Gospels can be exceptions, however—if you marked every reference to Jesus, the page would be covered!).

Remember, the reason we're studying in the first place is to behold the glory of our God. Marking key words can seem like a rather unspiritual way to do that, but by noticing and marking everything the Bible says about God, you can learn about him—and that's the main point of serious Bible study.

Making Lists

The point of marking key words is to learn more about them, to see how they relate to the rest of the text, and ultimately to understand what the author is trying to say. That's why we make lists about them. Writing down what you observe about God, sin, or faith from a given passage can open up new insights about that subject. It gives you a chance to slow down and learn more about the main point the author is making.

Once you've marked every place a key word is used, you're ready to make a list about it. Find every spot on the page where you marked that word (or a pronoun or synonym), and then write down what you observe about the key word from that verse.

As you do this, keep in mind our observation questions: *Who? What? When? Where? Why? How?* You don't have to write down answers to all of these questions for every word. Just keep them in the back of your head. Develop a mind-set of asking questions and finding out everything you can about the text.

As you write down what you observe about these key words, try to stick to the wording of the text. That's not to say you should never paraphrase, but using the words the author used helps you make sure you're adhering to the text—not adding your own interpretation or what you think it should mean.

Let's go back to our example of Psalm 71. One key word in this psalm is "righteousness." It's used five times in the chapter. My list for "righteousness" would look like this:

Righteousness
- God's righteousness is what will cause him to deliver the psalmist (v. 2).
- The psalmist's mouth will tell of God's righteousness all day long because he doesn't even know its sum (i.e., it can't be measured) (v. 15).
- The psalmist will make mention of God's righteousness alone (v. 16).
- God's righteousness reaches to the heavens (v. 19).
- The psalmist's tongue will utter God's righteousness all day long (v. 24).

See how much you can learn about God's righteousness, just from this one chapter? It can't be measured, it's bigger than anything we can imagine, it's the reason God delivers his people, and it's the object of our praise!

This could also help you discover the main point of the psalm: God is righteous—he does what is right. It's part of his nature. His righteousness is what the psalmist appeals to when he needs deliverance. And God's righteousness, unlike ours, never fails. You can trust in it completely. It never ends or runs out. So when the psalmist says, "God, don't forsake me! Save me!" you know he's trusting that the righteous God will answer his prayer. This psalm is a cry for help, but also an expression of great faith in God.

Making Lists about Our Maker

We talked about how you'll usually mark references to God. When you make lists, make sure you write down everything you observe about God from your marked references of him. Here's an example list for God in Psalm 71:

- We can take refuge in him (v. 1).
- He is righteous to deliver and rescue (v. 2).
- He gave the command to save the psalmist (v. 3).
- He is a rock and a fortress (v. 3).
- He was the psalmist's hope and trust (v. 5).
- He sustained the psalmist from birth and took him from his mother's womb (v. 6).
- He is a strong refuge (v. 7).
- The psalmist's mouth was filled with his praise and glory (v. 8).
- His righteous acts and deeds of salvation are uncountable (v. 15).
- He does mighty deeds (v. 16).
- He is righteous (v. 16).
- He taught the psalmist from his youth (v. 17).
- He does wondrous deeds (v. 17).
- He has might and power (v. 18).
- His righteousness reaches to the heavens (v. 19).
- He has done great things (v. 19).
- There is no one like him (v. 19).

- He made the psalmist see troubles but would revive him again (v. 20).
- He is faithful (v. 22).
- He redeemed the soul of the psalmist (v. 23).

Remember—the Bible is all about God. The ultimate end of our study should be to see him and delight in who he is. Making lists doesn't seem very worshipful or spiritual; it seems academic. But as you write down everything the text says about God, you'll see more clearly who he is. Aspects of his character that you never noticed may pop out to you. In writing everything down, you'll get a chance to slow down and meditate on God's character and works.

In fact, you might want to set aside a day or two of study just for this. Spend some time writing down everything the text says about God, and then meditate on the truths you discover. Pray them back to God—use the words of the Bible to praise him for who he is, confess any sins you've been convicted of, thank him for what he's done, and bring any requests to him in faith.

What the Author Said

The Bible isn't some mystical book that can mean whatever we want or need it to mean at any given moment. It was written by real people, in a real place and time, and those people had very real things they were trying to say.

Observation is about discovering exactly what it was they were saying. Observation questions, key words, and lists aren't magical methods that bring out something that wasn't there before. They're tools to help us see what's already there—what the author said.

As you observe, keep that perspective in mind. It's easy to get caught up in all the details of inductive study, but if we devote ourselves to writing things down and making lists without keeping the big picture in mind, we've missed it.

How?

Inductive study is a tool that serves a purpose—and that purpose is to see what the Bible is saying, understand what it means, and apply it to our lives.

QUESTIONS

Welcome back to your study of 3 John! Come to God in prayer, and then let's begin.

Overview

1. Read through the book of 3 John again. What is the main theme of this book?

2. What can you learn about the author and recipient? Who wrote this book? To whom was it written? What does the book tell you about them?

3. Scholars believe 3 John was written by the apostle John. Write what you observe about John from the following references:

   • Matthew 4:21–22

   • Matthew 17:1; 26:37

   • Mark 3:17

   • Revelation 1:1–2, 9

4. This book doesn't have a clear statement of purpose. From what the author talks about, can you deduce the reason it was written?

Observation Questions

5. Now start asking questions and find the answers.

- What people are mentioned? (And who are they?)

- What two people are contrasted in verses 9–12?

- What is Gaius doing (vv. 3, 5)?

- What is Diotrephes doing (vv. 9, 10)?

- What two things are contrasted in verse 11?

- What does Demetrius have (v. 12)?

- When does the elder hope to see Gaius (v. 14)?

- Why is the elder glad (v. 3)?

How?

- Why should we support our brothers and sisters who go out for the sake of God's name (v. 8)?

- How is Gaius walking and acting (vv. 3, 5)?

Key Words
6. Mark the following key words, then make a list of what you learn about each:

- God

- love

- truth

- good

- evil

Summary
7. Briefly summarize what you've observed from your study so far.

10

INTERPRETATION:

"WHAT DOES IT MEAN?"

What do you do when you can't understand something?

It might be a math problem, a tool, a piece of machinery, or even a road map. Whatever it is, it's the first time you look at it, and you have no idea what to make of it. What do you do?

Most likely, you try and figure it out yourself. You read the problem over and over, look up terms and instructions on the Internet, or use your prior knowledge of geography to puzzle through it. Hopefully, by the time you're done, you'll have come up with the answer to the math problem or figured out where the map is taking you.

But, if you're still lost, the next thing you'll do is ask for help. It might be your parent, a teacher, or a friend (or, if you're like me, the GPS system on your phone). What's unclear to you will hopefully be obvious to them. They can help you complete that math problem, understand those operation instructions, or follow the road map to wherever you're going.

This is a little bit like the process of interpretation.

How?

We've been reading and "overviewing" and discovering context and asking questions and marking key words and making lists. We've learned a lot about the author, the recipients, the text, what the author is saying, the ideas we're dealing with, and most of all—about God.

But as you were studying, didn't you occasionally run across something that made you shake your head? Was there a word or a verse that made you frown and say, "I really don't understand"?

Interpretation is where we get to address those questions. This is where we get to dig down deep and figure out what exactly that word or verse or passage *means*.

NO ONE-SIZE-FITS-ALL

This is the fun part. It's also the hard part.

Interpretation is less method-driven than observation. There's no, "If you do these five steps in this particular order, you'll know what the passage means." There are tools you can use, of course—that's what this chapter is all about! But how you use those tools is going to be directed by your own study skills and the guidance of the Holy Spirit.

There's no one-size-fits-all approach to interpretation; the way you come at it will look different depending on your situation, your study style, the amount of time you have, and which book you're studying.

- You can just focus on the things you don't understand in each passage or chapter. This approach works well when you have less time, or when you're studying something like a narrative.
- You can work through it verse by verse, digging deep into the meaning of each phrase. With a shorter book, or one that's packed full of doctrine, this type of in-depth study can be invaluable.

- You can focus on the passage as a whole. This can be helpful if the entire passage is confusing, especially if it's something like prophecy.
- You can pick a section of each chapter and "camp out" there, focusing in on those few verses for deeper study. Again, this works well with narrative.

In this chapter, I'm not going to focus on a particular one of these or give a set method for interpretation. I'm just going to lay out some of the tools you'll probably find helpful as you work to understand the meaning of the text.

Again, don't neglect prayer and reliance on God. He's the one who wrote this word—it would be foolishness not to run to him again and again with our questions, our frailty, and our lack of understanding. Take them to him and allow him to sustain you with his wisdom and strength.

UNDERSTANDING THE FLOW OF THOUGHT

How do these two ideas relate to each other? Why would the author include that paragraph? Why did he just switch topics so fast?

It can be confusing when there's no apparent connection between one verse and the next. However, the biblical authors didn't usually skip around from one topic to a completely separate one (with the exception being parts of Proverbs). If the two ideas seem unrelated, they're probably not. We just need to understand the author's flow of thought.

First, make sure you have a handle on the big ideas of the book, especially the purpose. Why is the author writing this? In an epistle, what specific problem is he dealing with? For instance, in Galatians, Paul is refuting the idea that Gentiles needed to become Jews and follow the law in order to be saved. Without that understanding (which comes from the first stages of observation!), much of the book will be confusing. But once you understand that, it's easier to see how things connect.

Second, look at the context. What was the author saying in the previous paragraph? The last chapter? Remember that chapter divisions were added long after the books of the Bible were written—sometimes the beginning of one chapter is just a continuation of the train of thought from the previous one.

For example, James 4 has a lot of different instructions (submit to God . . . don't speak against one another . . . don't boast about what you're going to do) that at first glance don't seem to fit together. But it all makes a lot more sense when you look at the end of chapter 3. James describes two different kinds of wisdom—the wisdom of men (bitter jealousy and selfish ambition), and the wisdom of God (pure, peaceable, gentle, reasonable, etc.). Looking at James 4 again, you can see how James contrasts the two, pointing out how his readers are exhibiting earthly wisdom through their "quarrels and fights" (v. 1), and how God calls them to submit to him in humility.

Sometimes the author's flow of thought can simply be obscured because of confusing grammar. In many of Paul's letters, he uses long, complex, twisting sentences. If you want to understand the cause-and-effect relationships, you almost have to read the sentence backward. Consider these verses from Colossians:

> We always thank God, the Father of our Lord Jesus Christ, when we pray for you, since we heard of your faith in Christ Jesus and of the love that you have for all the saints, because of the hope laid up for you in heaven. Of this you have heard before in the word of the truth, the gospel, which has come to you, as indeed in the whole world it is bearing fruit and increasing—as it also does among you, since the day you heard it and understood the grace of God in truth. (Col. 1:3–6)

That's all *two* sentences! This is just the introduction to the book, and it's already packed full of theology (and difficult grammar).

This is where *paraphrasing* can be helpful. You may have done something like this for school: read part of a book, then restate it in your own words. The act of putting something into words yourself forces you to clarify it in your own mind. Similar to observation questions, paraphrasing helps you spend time in the passage and work through it. In this case, it can help you understand the flow of the author's thought.

My paraphrase of this passage would probably look something like this:

- The gospel is constantly bearing fruit and increasing throughout the world (v. 6).
- The gospel has come to the Colossians (v. 6).
- They heard of the gospel and understood the grace of God in truth (v. 6).
- The gospel is constantly bearing fruit and increasing in them (v. 6).
- In the gospel they heard of the hope laid up for them in heaven (v. 5).
- This hope inspires their faith in Christ Jesus and their love for all the saints (v. 4).
- Their faith in Christ and love for the saints cause Paul and Timothy (cf. v. 1) to give thanks to God and pray always for the Colossians (v. 3).

See how understanding the cause-and-effect—the *why* and *how* of this passage—helps you to see the flow and meaning? Each thought is dependent on the next. By writing them out in reverse, I can see that Paul is focusing primarily on the gospel: the gospel is what is bearing fruit in the Colossians, and it's producing the hope that inspires their faith in Christ and love for others, which in turn inspires Paul and Timothy to give thanks and pray for them.

This, by the way, is an example of how observation and interpretation can collide. In a sense, much of what we just did here is observation because we're trying to discover what the passage is really *saying*. But we're also trying to discover its *meaning* at the same time—that makes it interpretation.

INTERPRETING SCRIPTURE THROUGH CROSS-REFERENCES

The heart of inductive Bible study is letting Scripture interpret itself. When we don't understand something, we shouldn't go first to what other people say it means. We should see if the Bible will tell us what it means.

The first place to look, of course, is the context. The surrounding verses and the overall purpose of the book will often give us the key to unlock a passage's meaning.

But sometimes we need to look further. That's where cross-references come in.

Cross-references are simply other parts of Scripture that relate to the passage you're studying. They can shed light on its interpretation, or expand on what you already know, or show you another facet of meaning you didn't see before.

This might be my favorite part of Bible study. I love getting to see those connections to other parts of Scripture. I love how cross-references gradually light up a passage, little by little increasing my understanding of God's word.

Going on a Treasure Hunt

But how do we find these cross-references? If you've been studying the Bible for a long time, you'll probably be able to see how what you're currently studying relates to something you've studied in the past. If you've memorized a lot of Scripture, you'll be able to make even more connections. But unless you have the entire Bible memorized, you probably won't be able to pull every relevant reference straight out of your head.

Thankfully, we don't have to rely on our own memories and knowledge. Many great scholars and Bible students have paved the way for us, and we have lots of tools at our disposal.

The first place to look is actually in the pages of your Bible. Look at your Bible. Do you have footnotes, or notes in the margins or down the center of the page? Much of the time, these will include cross-references. Here is an example of what it might look like in John 3:16.

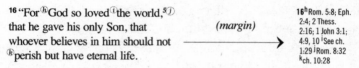

¹⁶ "For [ⓚ]God so loved [ⓘ]the world,^{5ⓙ} that he gave his only Son, that whoever believes in him should not [ⓚ]perish but have eternal life. *(margin)* ———→ 16 ^hRom. 5:8; Eph. 2:4; 2 Thess. 2:16; 1 John 3:1; 4:9, 10 ⁱSee ch. 1:29 ^jRom. 8:32 ^kch. 10:28

Illustration 10.1: Cross-Reference Example[1]

Another great resource for finding cross-references is called the *Treasury of Scripture Knowledge* (or *TSK*). You can get it in book form, but it's also available (free) on Blue Letter Bible and other websites. *TSK* takes every verse in the Bible and lists the references of verses that relate to it. Often you'll even be able to find related verses for each individual phrase.

Cross Referencing John the Baptist

Not every cross-reference you find will relate to what you're studying or answer the questions you have about the text. Look at each one, and if it does relate, write down the reference in your notebook with a (brief) summary of the verse or how it sheds light on the passage.

For an example, let's look at John 1:29. Here John the Baptist is speaking. In context, the author, John the apostle (different John!), has been talking about how Jesus is the Word made flesh, God himself. He also narrates how John the Baptist told the religious leaders he wasn't the Christ, but the one preparing the way for him.

> The next day he [John the Baptist] saw Jesus coming to him and said, "Behold, the Lamb of God, who takes away the sin of the world!" (John 1:29)

What stands out to you in this verse? The first thing I notice is that John calls Jesus the "Lamb of God." This is important, because chapter 1 of John is introducing Jesus and telling us who he is. When Jesus actually appears on the scene, this is the first thing said about him. That should make us listen!

So what does it mean that Jesus is the "Lamb of God"? When I look up this verse and phrase in *TSK*, I find lots of cross-references (over thirty, just for this one phrase!). I certainly wouldn't write them all down, but a few stick out.

- Genesis 22:7–8: God had commanded Abraham to sacrifice his son Isaac on an altar, but here Abraham tells Isaac that God will provide the lamb for the burnt offering.
- Exodus 12:3–13: When God passed through the land of Egypt to strike down every firstborn son, he provided a way for Israel to be spared: a *spotless, unblemished lamb* had to be killed, and the blood was to be painted on the doorposts as a sign. This was the first Passover.
- Isaiah 53:7: This is a prophecy that the coming Savior would be like a *lamb led to slaughter*.
- 1 Peter 1:19: We have been redeemed with precious blood, *like the blood of a spotless lamb*.

In the Old Testament, we see again and again the symbolism of a lamb being killed to save someone from death. The lamb would die in a person's place. In the New Testament, we learn that, like the lamb, Jesus Christ was killed in our place. His blood redeemed us. He was killed to take the wrath of God on our behalf and to give us his record of perfect righteousness.

If you keep reading in John, you'll see Passover imagery used throughout. In fact, it was no accident that Jesus was crucified at the time of the Passover (John 13:1). He was the true Savior, and all the Passover lambs throughout the centuries had pointed to him.

Into His Image

Let's do one more example, just to show the different ways we can use the tool of cross referencing.

In 1 John 3:2, John writes, "Beloved, we are God's children now, and what we will be has not yet appeared; but we know that when he appears we shall be like him, because we shall see him as he is."

What does it mean that "when he appears, we shall be like him"? We know, based on Scripture, that it doesn't mean we'll become gods—that would be blasphemous, not to mention impossible. Again, *TSK* has lots of cross-references for this verse, and you might want to look at them sometime. It's an exciting subject! Here are a few I would write down if I were studying this passage:

- "For this light momentary affliction is preparing for us an eternal weight of glory far beyond all comparison" (2 Cor. 4:17).
- "When Christ who is your life appears, then you also will appear with him in glory" (Col. 3:4).
- "[Christ] will transform our lowly body to be like his glorious body, by the power that enables him even to subject all things to himself" (Phil. 3:21).
- "And after my skin has been thus destroyed, yet in my flesh I shall see God" (Job 19:26).

- "And we all, with unveiled face, beholding the glory of the Lord, are being transformed into the same image from one degree of glory to another. For this comes from the Lord who is the Spirit" (2 Cor. 3:18).

What do we learn from these verses? First of all, we see that this life isn't all there is—we will live for eternity. Here we also find the doctrine of resurrection: in the end, believers will be raised from the dead and given new, glorious bodies. Most importantly, we will see Jesus. "Yet in my flesh I shall see God," Job said. We will look on the face of our Lord with our physical eyes.

Finally, we learn something very beautiful: seeing God, truly looking at his glory, transforms us. First John 3:2 says, "We shall be like him, *because* we shall see him as he is." That has glorious implications for Bible study! We see God's glory in his word, as in a mirror, and we're being "transformed into the same image from one degree of glory to another" (2 Cor. 3:18). Little by little, we become more like him.

These examples barely scratch the surface of what we can learn from cross-references. Even though the Bible is made up of so many different books, it's still all one story. All the books were inspired by the same God. That means they all relate to each other, and one book is very often necessary to explain another.

GREEK AND HEBREW WORD STUDIES

When you read the Bible, you probably read it in whatever language you grew up speaking. I read it in English. As we discussed back in chapter 2, there are many different translations to choose from, and they all have their own strengths and weaknesses.

But the Bible wasn't written in English, or any other language we speak today. The whole reason we have so many translations is that the Bible was written in a different language many centuries ago, and just as with any translation, there are multiple ways to render the same meanings in our own tongue.

Sometimes, however, the Greek and Hebrew carry meanings that don't quite translate into our own language at all. Sometimes we don't have a word that exactly corresponds to the original. Sometimes two or three words that are different in the original text all translate to the same word in our Bible—thereby losing subtle shades of meaning.

It would make things a lot easier if we could just read the Bible in the original languages, wouldn't it? Well, yes, but if you're thinking that takes a lot of work, you're right. Pastors and Bible teachers learn ancient Greek and Hebrew in seminary, and it takes several semesters. Most of us don't have access to that kind of education.

However, there are some tools to help us understand what words the original authors used, and what they mean. Remember that Greek and Hebrew are not the end-all solution to our problems of interpretation. Just learning the original words won't unlock every meaning of the text. However, they can help us understand more clearly what the biblical authors meant.

Strong Language

My family keeps a very large book on the shelf in our office. It's one of the thickest, heaviest books we own. I've always thought it would be the first thing I'd grab in the case of an intruder; it's so heavy it could be a weapon!

That book is called *Strong's Exhaustive Concordance of the Bible*. It takes every English word used in the King James Bible and lists them alphabetically. Then, under each word, it lists the references to *every single time* that word is used in the entire Bible. Next to each of those references is a number—that's the number assigned to the Greek or Hebrew word used in that particular verse.

How?

At the back of the book is a dictionary section where all those numbers are listed in order—the Hebrew words (Old Testament) first, and then the Greek (New Testament) after. By each number is the corresponding word in Hebrew or Greek, with a pronunciation in English letters and a short definition.

M'r 10:21 Jesus beholding him him, and said 25
Lu 7:47 many are forgiven: for she *l'* much: "
Joh 3:16 For God so *l'* the world   "
        19 men *l'* darkness rather than light.   "
     11: 5 Now Jesus *l'* Martha, and her sister. "

25. ἀγαπάω agapaō, *ag-ap-ah'-o*; perhaps from ἄγαν ágan (*much*) (or compare H5689); to love (in a social or moral sense):—(be-)love(-ed). Compare G3568.

Illustration 10.2: *Strong's* Example[2]

This makes it relatively easy to look up a word in the original language. If you were studying John, for instance, and wanted to see what word is used for "loved" in John 3:16 ("for God so *loved* the world . . ."), you would look up the word "loved" in the concordance section. Then you would go down until you found "John 3:16," and see what number is used. You would find that the number is 25, and by flipping back to the dictionary section, you would discover that the Greek word used is *agapao*. The definition is simply, "to love (in a social or moral sense)."

If you don't have a physical copy of *Strong's* (or if that sounds really time-consuming!), you can use an online Bible or Bible app. It's easy to find and generally free to use. These often include an interlinear tool (a tool that lists the Greek words of the passage next to their English counterparts), so all you need to do is click on the verse you're studying and find the word you want to look up.

The Righteousness of God

Let's look at another example to see what kinds of things we can learn from the original language. Remember our key word from Psalm 71, "righteousness"? If you wanted to better understand how God's righteousness is so important to the psalmist's cry for help and his confidence, you could look it up in the Hebrew to see what the word means.

When we look up verse 14 using an interlinear tool, we see that the Hebrew word is *tsedaqah*. The basic *Strong's* definition is "rightness." God is righteous—that means he does and is what is right. It's very basic, but already it helps us get a better understanding of this word we use all the time.

If we wanted a further definition, we could look up the word in a lexicon or Bible dictionary. A lexicon contains each Greek or Hebrew word, arranged by their respective alphabets. A Bible dictionary (such as *Vine's*) will arrange each Greek or Hebrew word under its English translation. When using one of these, it's important to remember to look for the reference of the verse you're studying. A dictionary or lexicon will give the different shades of meaning for each use of the word, as sometimes a word can mean different things in different passages.

From the entry for *tsedaqah* in *Thayer's Lexicon*, we learn that it means the following: "justice, as of a king, of God, as shown both in punishing the wicked and in freeing, vindicating, and rewarding the godly."

Can you see why the psalmist appeals to God's righteousness in Psalm 71? He knows that God is a God who does what is right—specifically, he punishes the wicked while "freeing, vindicating, and rewarding" those who follow him. Based on this, the psalmist knows he can trust God to keep his promises to deliver him and to punish the wicked who are persecuting him.

We can learn a lot from looking up words in the original languages. However, that doesn't mean we always have to use this tool. If all this just sounds very complicated and confusing, feel free to not worry about it for now. It's certainly possible to study the Bible without delving into the Hebrew and Greek words, and it's often better to get some practice with basic study methods before attempting to look at the original languages.

QUESTIONS AND COMMENTARIES

We've mentioned commentaries a few times before, but now is when we get to really use them.

Remember, commentaries should be saved until *after* you've studied the passage thoroughly for yourself. That's not just because it would be "cheating," or for the sake of having a challenge. It's because before we go to other people's interpretations of the Bible, we need to see what it means for ourselves. Once you know the passage, you'll be able to judge any other interpretation by how well it matches your studies of the text.

Once you have studied it for yourself, however, the insights of other wise Christians can be invaluable. The pastors and teachers who write good commentaries have spent years studying the Bible. They have a broad and deep knowledge of God's word, and they're experienced at observation, interpretation, and application.

You might choose to look up commentary on a verse you still don't understand, even after you've studied it, or you might just read the entire commentary. Either way, as you're reading, compare everything to what you've studied. Does it match up with Scripture? If the commentator presents an interpretation different from yours, carefully compare both to the text. There are some passages that are hard to understand, and many strong Christians and excellent Bible students have different interpretations. Thinking through them can help strengthen your own faith and understanding of God's word.

Your home or church likely has some good Bible commentaries, and many are also available online. See Appendix A for suggestions.

SUMMING IT ALL UP

Are you beginning to see just how deep and rich God's word is? There's so much more than we could ever begin to discover just from skimming the surface.

At this point you've learned to discover what the text *says* and what it *means*. But there's one very important step we haven't covered yet—*applying* it to our own lives. That's what we'll cover in the next chapter.

QUESTIONS

1. Read through 3 John again, in order to keep everything in context. Read verses 9–12 again. Why does the author mention both Diotrephes and Demetrius? What is his point? (*Hint*—look at verse 11!).

2. How does this relate to "walking in the truth" from verses 3–4?

Cross-References

3. Look up the following cross-references for "walking in the truth" and write down your observations.

   • 1 Kings 3:6

   • Psalm 26:1–3

   • Galatians 2:11–14

   • 2 John 1:4–6

4. Now it's your turn! Pick another verse or short passage from 3 John you'd like to study in-depth. Use the *Treasury of Scripture*

How?

Knowledge or the footnotes in your copy of the Scriptures to look up cross-references, and write down what you learn.

Greek Word Studies

5. Look up the Greek word for "truth" in 3 John 1:3 in a *Strong's* concordance or on BlueLetterBible.org. Write down the Strong's number, Greek word, and definition.

6. If you have *Vine's Expository Dictionary* or you're using Blue LetterBible.org, look up the definition of this word in *Vine's*. You'll have to look up the English word first, then find the correct *Strong's* number under it. Find the meaning that corresponds to 3 John 1:3 and write it out. What does this tell you about "walking in truth"?

7. Now it's your turn! What verse or passage did you decide to study further? Is there a key word there that might be easier to understand if you look it up in the Greek?

Further Questions and Commentaries

8. Do you have any questions about what you've been studying? Anything you'd like to explore further?

9. Find a commentary, whether in your home, at your church, or online. Write down what you learn and how it expands your understanding of 3 John. Was there any place you disagreed with the author of the commentary? Why?

11

APPLICATION:

"HOW DOES THIS CHANGE ME?"

Can you imagine if a character in a book were to read their own story? If Lucy read The Chronicles of Narnia or if Frodo read The Lord of the Rings? That would be awesome!

But what if they just read the story and said, "Hmm, that's interesting"? We would think they were incredibly foolish. How could they not care that this was *their* story? That it told them about themselves and the kind of world they lived in and what they should do and what was going to happen?

We're characters in this cosmic story that the author of history is writing. God has graciously let us see not only our place in the story, but the entire sweep of the narrative. We're plodding along through a valley, but he's shown us the map, and we know what's on the other side of the mountains. We've seen what it all means, where we've come from, where we're going, and the purpose of it all.

That's why we can't treat Bible study as just an intellectual exercise. We can't let our learning end at mere knowledge. J. I. Packer writes,

> [If] we pursue theological knowledge for its own sake, it is bound to go bad on us. . . . To be preoccupied with getting theological knowledge as an end in itself, to approach Bible study with no higher a motive than a desire to know all the answers, is the direct route to a state of self-satisfied self-deception.[1]

The Bible isn't just something we study for history or literature class. It's not just information. It's not there to help us pass a test, complete a class, improve our lives, or look better in the eyes of others. It's "living and active, sharper than any two-edged sword" (Heb. 4:12). It's "profitable for teaching, for reproof, for correction, and for training in righteousness" (2 Tim. 3:16). It's meant to do something in us. It's meant to change us.

When we look at this true, overarching story, when we see the glory of God in Scripture, when we see what he says about us and his will for our lives, we shouldn't just say, "Hmm, that's interesting." We need to be taking it to heart, letting it change the way we think and speak and live right here and now.

That's application.

THE WRONG KIND OF APPLICATION

When I was a lot younger, I read my Bible every day.

That wasn't a bad thing obviously. The bad part was the way I did it.

You see, my idea of Bible reading was to read a chapter and then ask what it told me to do. What moral lessons could I take from it?

As I read through the Gospels, that was pretty easy. There are lots of commands and exhortations in the Gospels: "Love your neighbor as yourself," "Seek first the kingdom of God," or "Forgive one another." I would read a chapter, find a lesson or a command to follow, close my Bible, and go about my day (most of the time without a thought for the lesson or command).

That worked pretty well—until I got to the end of Luke. The part about the crucifixion.

I finished the chapter and asked myself the same question I always did: *How does this apply to me?* Well, there weren't many commands in that chapter. But I did see one lesson to take away— you shouldn't mock people, like the Jews were mocking Jesus on the cross. Mocking was bad.

Then it hit me like a bag of cement. *That wasn't what the chapter was about.* Not remotely. I had just taken one of the most central, shocking, horrifying, glorious narratives in history and reduced it to an innocuous moral lesson.

Sadly, that's too often how we approach God's word. We read it, and our first question is, "What am I supposed to do? What commands should I be following?" We put the focus squarely on ourselves.

Don't get me wrong. I don't mean that we shouldn't follow the Bible's commands. But following rules is *not* the main point of Scripture. If the Bible is no more than a bunch of rules, then it's no different from any other world religion or self-improvement handbook—except that these rules are impossible to follow.

We can make the opposite mistake too. It's all too easy to swing the other direction—to read the Bible looking only for promises and encouragement. The Bible is full of promises, comfort, and assurance. But again, if they're divorced from the bigger story, they're meaningless. Just like when we only look for commands and moral lessons, if we focus only on the parts that make us feel good, we remove God's glory from the picture and put the focus on ourselves.

How?

We get application wrong when we try to make the Bible primarily about *us*—about who *we* are and what *we* should do. But it's not about us—it's about God.

WHO IS THE PROTAGONIST?

Remember the protagonist, from chapter 3? The protagonist of the story is the main character. It's the one around whom the story revolves.

If we're honest, we want to be the protagonists of our own stories. We want everything to revolve around us. We want people to look at us and see how wonderful we are. That's the reality behind so much of what we do, whether the things we say or the way we dress or the friends we choose.

But the Bible tells a different kind of story. Remember the metanarrative? In that story—the true story—God is the main character. He created us, and then when we sinned, he gave everything to save us (his enemies) and restore creation to its original order.

We aren't the protagonist in this story. We're not the hero; we're not the innocent victim; in fact, we're not even the villain. We're just the unworthy recipients of God's unfathomable grace and mercy.

When we approach application as if it's all about figuring out what we can do better and how to improve ourselves—or as if it's all about boosting our self-esteem—we get it completely wrong. We're trying to set ourselves up as the protagonist.

The point of the Bible isn't to tell us how to keep a lot of rules but to tell us about God. And *why?* So we can have a relationship with him. He is to be the center of our life, the object of all our love and affection.

As we read and study our Bible, this is what we have to pursue. We don't approach our study with a mind-set of legalism (trying to do enough good or keep enough rules to earn God's favor). We

160

don't approach it with a mind-set of wanting to make ourselves feel better. We approach it with a desire to learn more about God so we can have a closer, deeper relationship with him.

WHITE-HOT WORSHIP

This is what John Piper says about the goal of Bible reading:

> Our ultimate goal in reading the Bible is *that God's infinite worth and beauty would be exalted in the everlasting, white-hot worship of the blood-bought Bride of Christ from every people, language, tribe, and nation.*[2]

The goal of Bible reading and study is worship. Not finding more rules to follow. Not finding reasons to feel good about ourselves. The goal is to see God in all his glory and to enjoy him.

We need to both see his glory with our minds and enjoy it with our hearts. It's a little like watching a thunderstorm roll in, a mountain range of clouds slowly taking over the sky while gusts of wind swirl around and pelt you with drops of water. You wouldn't just nod and acknowledge it. You stand in awe (and maybe a little fear) of the storm's beauty and power. The Scriptures are full of commands to delight in God. Psalm 34:8 exhorts us to "*taste and see* that the LORD is good." Jesus himself said that he gave his words for our *joy* (John 15:11). The goal of all our Bible study is to see who God is, and as we see him, to enjoy him—his presence, who he is, and what he has done for us in the gospel.

Application, then, is *not* primarily about us. Yes, it has to do with us—it answers the question, "What does this mean for me? What is my place in this story?" But it's primarily about seeing God and enjoying his glory.

As David Mathis says, "Coming to the Scriptures to see and feel makes for a drastically different approach than primarily coming to do."[3] We need to reorient our application away from a me-centered approach and toward a God-centered approach.

How?

BEHOLD AND BE TRANSFORMED

This has massive implications for how we practically go about our Bible study. In fact, it can change our entire approach to the Bible.

It's important to realize, however, that seeing God's glory and delighting in him doesn't just end there, inside our hearts. It's supposed to change us. Remember what we talked about in chapter 5? Spending time with God and learning about him leads to growing love and faith, and this changes how we act toward others.

Worship begins within us. But it doesn't end there. The sight of God's glory and the knowledge of his love slowly shape and mold our hearts into his own image. And that glory—which is now residing within and reflecting from our hearts—shines outward to touch every person around us.

My friend Jaquelle Crowe says that "the gospel changes everything"—from our identity to our relationships to our view of God's church.[4] This is what we're pursuing in application: this inside-out change that begins at the heart level with the knowledge of God himself. As we *behold* God's glory in Scripture, we will be *transformed* into his image at a heart level, which will result in visible *obedience* to his commands.

WHAT DOES APPLICATION LOOK LIKE?

If interpretation is less method-driven than observation, application is even less systematic. In fact, it's hard to really talk about method here.

Application is something that rises out of both observation and interpretation. Don't restrict it to one area of your study. Interpretation might naturally lead to application as the third step in the order of inductive study—but you might also be struck by some awesome aspect of God's character or work in the very first steps of observation.

As you work through observation and interpretation, prayerfully consider what you learn. Look for what it tells you about God and how it connects to the bigger story of God's glory and redeeming work.

Don't neglect the commands and promises of God either. Even while they're not the first or only thing we should look for, they're still essential. Allow God's word to convict and comfort you. Ponder the glorious descriptions of God in Isaiah, the difficult imperatives in James, and the beautiful promises of Psalms. Praise him for who he is, and pray for strength to obey his commands and trust in his promises.

Don't just rush through your study, learning facts and writing down information so you can get to the next part of your day. Slow down. Think and pray about what you're learning. Ask God to show you more about himself, and let it change you. "Turn each truth that [you] learn *about* God into matter for meditation *before* God, leading to prayer and praise *to* God."[5]

MEDITATE DAY AND NIGHT

This process of slowing down and thinking about the truths you're learning is also known as meditation. It's essential for applying God's word to our lives. However, the idea can seem strange, foreign, or even frightening. What exactly does it mean? How do we go about it?

Before we go any further, let me assure you: this section has nothing to do with Eastern rituals or New Age spirituality. Meditation is a biblical discipline centered around God's word, and it's crucial as we seek to become more like Christ.

The Scriptures repeatedly call for meditation on God and his word. The most famous passage is in Psalm 1.

> Blessed is the man
> who walks not in the counsel of the wicked,

> nor stands in the way of sinners,
>> nor sits in the seat of scoffers;
> but his delight is in the law of the LORD,
>> and on his law he meditates day and night.
>
> He is like a tree
>> planted by streams of water
> that yields its fruit in its season,
>> and its leaf does not wither.
> In all that he does, he prospers. (Ps. 1:1–3)

Meditation, according to this passage, leads to flourishing. So what exactly is it? Simply, it's the process of "chewing" on God's word. It's dwelling on a particular verse or scriptural truth and letting it move you to wonder at God. J. I. Packer defines it this way:

> Meditation is the activity of calling to mind, and thinking over, and dwelling on, and applying to oneself, the various things that one knows about the works and ways and purposes and promises of God. It is an activity of holy thought, consciously performed in the presence of God, under the eye of God, by the help of God, as a means of communion with God. Its purpose is to clear one's mental and spiritual vision of God, and to let his truth make its full and proper impact on one's mind and heart.[6]

What a great God we serve, that he would allow us to have such communion with him! That he would let us know him and spend time in his presence!

Application begins with seeing and worshiping God. That means this kind of meditation is essential to our study. Meditation takes the truth we're learning with our mind and imprints it on our heart. It lets us draw closer to God as we take the time to behold him.

As you study, then, watch for these truths about God. It could be a single verse that jumps out at you, or it could be a broader principle. Take some time to pause, think it over, and dwell on it. Let it lead you into prayer, whether praise, confession, requests, or all three.

Don't hurry through your study. It's better to do less studying and take time to meditate and pray than to have a very productive study session that includes no time to reflect on what you've learned. Marking key words, writing down lists, and looking up cross-references are all helpful and important parts of Bible study. But, like all roads once led to Rome, each of these disciplines should be a path leading us to the golden city of meditation, where we can dwell on God's truth and live in the midst of wonders.

TAKE IT WITH YOU

The Bible is meant to invade your life. Every aspect—from waking to school to work to Bible study to sports to social media to church to movies to bedtime—should be informed and transformed by the truth of the gospel.

The psalmists exhort us to meditate on God's word day and night. That means all the time. When we get up from our Bible study—whenever and wherever that is—we can't leave behind what we've learned. We have to take it with us into the various kinds of work and rest that make up each day.

That means we're going to have to memorize it.

I've found Bible memory is intimidating to a lot of people: "Oh, I have a terrible memory," or "I don't have time for that." It's understandable—especially if we have a mind-set of achievement and lists. If we think Bible memory requires complicated methods and review schedules, we might be too intimidated to even try.

But what if that's not what Bible memory is really about? What if, as David Mathis says, it's "a tool in the belt of meditation"?[7]

Memorizing the Scriptures is vital to our Christian walk. That doesn't necessarily mean you need to memorize the entire Bible, or even huge tracts of it. It does mean we need to be diligent about treasuring it in our hearts (Ps. 119:11).

Having Scripture inside you, ready to hand, will prove invaluable for the discipline of meditation. You'll be able to pull it out anytime your brain isn't busy, in the little breaths of air and the in-between spaces of waiting that punctuate our busy lives.

Start small. As you're studying, you'll likely come across a verse that jumps out to you—something that encapsulates the meaning of the passage, encourages your heart, or inspires wonder at God. Make it your goal to memorize that verse. Write it out on a piece of paper or make it the lock screen on your phone. Repeat it to yourself several times.

Then meditate on that verse throughout the day. Think about each phrase and what it means (this will also help you imprint it on your mind, so you remember it better!). My mom likes to repeat a verse to herself over and over, each time emphasizing a different word. Use your memorized Scripture as an opportunity to think about the truth when you're doing chores, driving to work, or sitting on the school bus.

Make Scripture a constant companion, an integral part of your life, letting memorization and meditation lead you again and again to prayer and praise. Allow it to change the way you think, feel, and act. This is the heart of application.

THE START OF THE JOURNEY

If you've ever been to a Christian summer camp, you know how inspirational it can be. Five or six days of being immersed in Scripture and biblical teaching can inspire you to live for God and renew your passion for him.

But then you have to come home. And once you get back into the rut of the everyday, it's hard to keep that zeal. It's all too easy to slowly fall away, becoming ensnared once again in apathy.

The reason for this is that a week-long experience once or twice a year is not enough to sustain our love for God. Just as life happens mostly in the unnoticed moments that come one after another, from school to work to free time, so does our spiritual growth. And that's where we need the Bible.

We've come a long way from chapter 1. We've laid out a theology of the Bible and discovered why it's possible (and necessary!) for teenagers to study it. We've gotten an overview of the Bible's metanarrative, looked at how it reveals God's will for us, and then seen how Scripture also helps us to fulfill those commands. We've also looked at the practical side of Bible study: where, when, and how to observe, interpret, and apply.

My hope and prayer is that this book has inspired you to a higher view of God's word and encouraged you to study it for yourself. But this is only the start of the journey.

What happens next—tomorrow and the day after and the week and month after that—is what's going to shape your life. Keep taking the next step, and the next, and the next. Transformation occurs as we take up God's word day after day after day. It's gradual. It's invisible. But God is working in you.

This journey is going to be hard sometimes, and you're going to feel like giving up. *Don't.* Keep following that road, praying for strength with every step. His word is our strength, our guide, and our light.

Remember—the end of the journey is coming; the end of the story, when we will be with the Lord and be made like him. Then we will be finally and totally at peace. We'll no longer need to see his glory in written words because we'll see his face. We'll no longer be traveling because we'll have arrived.

How?

Until then, "to him who is able to keep you from stumbling and to present you blameless before the presence of his glory with great joy, to the only God, our Savior, through Jesus Christ our Lord, be glory, majesty, dominion, and authority, before all time and now and forevermore. Amen" (Jude 24–25).

QUESTIONS

1. What do you generally think of when you hear the word *application*? Do you think of it differently now?

2. What are some practical steps you can take with regards to meditation and Scripture memory?

3. After studying 3 John, what verses or truths stick out to you? Has this book changed your thinking or shown you somewhere you need to grow? What did you learn about God?

Epilogue

SHELBY KENNEDY

A Life Transformed and a Legacy Left

Shelby Kennedy is one of my heroes.

She was a young woman who truly loved God with her heart, soul, and strength. She was passionate for him, and she extended that love to everyone around her—her family, her church, and people in the countries where she traveled on missions trips. She poured into Haitian children as well as her own siblings.

Shelby would say she wanted her life to be like a stone thrown into a pond—she wanted the ripples to expand into the lives of many others. She wanted to make a difference. She wanted to leave a legacy.[1]

I never met Shelby Kennedy. She died after a fierce battle with cancer several years ago—before I ever heard her name.

Shelby's family and friends wanted to honor her love for God, and particularly for his word. They started a foundation in her honor: the Shelby Kennedy Foundation. In 2009, this foundation sponsored the first-ever National Bible Bee Competition.

In the years of this competition's existence, hundreds of children and teens have competed at the national level—memorizing literally hundreds of Bible verses in the process. And thousands more participate each year at the local level.

That's thousands of minds and hearts that have been filled with Scripture. Thousands of lives that have been changed.

I know countless alumni and contestants who would affirm that their lives have been forever changed as a result of their participation in the competition. I know mine was. God's word does not return void, and it's had an immeasurable impact through the National Bible Bee.

We'll never know how deep and wide that impact truly is. It spans not just current contestants and alumni, but their families, their friends, their churches, those they witness to, and those they reach with their writing. You might never have held this book in your hands if not for Shelby Kennedy. I likely would never have written it.

Why do I say all this? To praise a single person or an organization? Not in the least. While Shelby, her family, and those who lead the Bible Bee deserve much respect, they're just an example. This is just one more instance of how God's word changes, transforms, and works in hearts and lives.

This has been happening throughout centuries, since Jesus's words and resurrection impelled a group of unlikely men and women to spread across the known world with a radical and life-transforming message of salvation. This is how entire cultures have been changed, churches planted, and lives turned around. This is the power of God through his written word.

So many of us want to leave a legacy. We want to make a difference. It starts with God's word making a difference in us.

Do you want your life to make an impact for God's glory? Do you want to leave a legacy of truth and love?

Then let it start on the inside. Immerse yourself in God's word. Devote yourself to knowing and loving your Savior, and allow your life to be transformed by truth.

Appendix A

RECOMMENDED RESOURCES

BIBLE STUDY AND THE SPIRITUAL DISCIPLINES

Arthur, Kay. *Lord, Teach Me to Study the Bible in 28 Days.* Eugene, OR: Harvest House, 2008.

Arthur, Kay, David Arthur, and Pete De Lacey. *The New How to Study Your Bible: Discover the Life-Changing Approach to God's Word.* Eugene, OR: Harvest House, 2010.

Mathis, David. *Habits of Grace: Enjoying Jesus through the Spiritual Disciplines.* Wheaton, IL: Crossway, 2016.

Wilkin, Jen. *Women of the Word: How to Study the Bible with Both Our Hearts and Our Minds.* Wheaton, IL: Crossway, 2014. This book is a great resource on Bible study for women and men alike!

BIBLE STUDY TOOLS

All of these are available online at BlueLetterBible.org.

Easton, M. G. *Easton's Bible Dictionary.* Orig. 1893.

Smith, William. *Smith's Bible Dictionary.* Peabody, MA: Hendrickson, 1990.

Strong, James. *Strong's Exhaustive Concordance of the Bible.* Peabody, MA: Hendrickson, 2009.

Torrey, R. A. *The Treasury of Scripture Knowledge.* Orig. 1830.

Vine, W. E. *Vine's Complete Expository Dictionary of Old and New Testament Words*. Nashville, TN: Thomas Nelson, 1996.

COMMENTARIES, SERMONS, AND TEACHING RESOURCES

I highly suggest you consult with your parents or pastor about which commentaries and other teaching materials they recommend. These are some resources I've found solid and helpful.

The Bible Knowledge Commentary. Edited by John F. Walvoord and Roy B. Zuck. Wheaton, IL: Scripture Press, 1985.

BiblicalStory.org. This site includes book-by-book commentaries and a video series on the Bible's metanarrative, available at http://the biblicalstory.org/.

DesiringGod.org. Sermons and messages by John Piper categorized by Scripture passage, available at https://www.desiringgod.org /scripture/with-messages.

Henry, Matthew. *Complete Commentary on the Bible*. 6 Vols. Orig. 1706. This is available online and in various print editions.

APOLOGETICS RESOURCES

AnswersinGenesis.org. Various resources on the creation-evolution debate, available at https://answersingenesis.org/.

Little, Paul E. *Know Why You Believe*. Downers Grove, IL: InterVarsity Press, 2008.

Piper, John. *A Peculiar Glory: How the Christian Scriptures Reveal Their Complete Truthfulness*. Wheaton, IL: Crossway, 2016.

Schaeffer, Francis. *He Is There and He Is Not Silent*. Vol. 1: *A Christian View of Philosophy and Culture* of *The Complete Works of Francis Schaeffer: A Christian Worldview*. 3rd ed. Wheaton, IL: Crossway, 1982.

SPIRITUAL GROWTH

Crowe, Jaquelle. *This Changes Everything: How the Gospel Transforms the Teen Years*. Wheaton, IL: Crossway, 2017.

Packer, J. I. *Knowing God*. Downers Grove, IL: InterVarsity Press, 1973.

TheRebelution.com. This is a website for teens by teens—helping teens to rebel against low expectations and to do hard things for the glory of God.

ELECTRONIC BIBLE RESOURCES

Blue Letter Bible. https://www.blueletterbible.org/.

YouVersion Bible App. This app offers hundreds of translations of the Bible in various languages, with the opportunity to listen to the Bible in addition to reading it.

Appendix B

MEMORIZATION TIPS AND HELPS

Bible memorization can be a daunting discipline to begin, but the rewards are more than worth the effort. Different methods work better for different people—don't feel bound to one specific way of doing it just because it works for someone else. Below I'll share several methods that I or others have found helpful. Try them out, experiment, and modify them to best fit you!

GENERAL TIPS

If you can, try to memorize something from the Bible book you're already studying. It's much easier to memorize something when you're intimately familiar with it through repeated reading and study.

Set a goal that's reasonable but also challenging. A chapter or favorite passage might be a good place to start. Give it a concrete timeframe too—commit to memorizing it within a week, a month, or some other period (a deadline can help you avoid the "I'll get to it later" excuse).

Memorize with others. Like Bible study, Bible memory flourishes in community. You can keep each other accountable and on track, not to mention share what you're learning.

Remember to review! When memorizing a longer Bible passage, make sure to review earlier verses. If you've chosen to memorize individual verses, set some kind of schedule to review older ones. You likely won't be able to keep every one of them memorized, but reviewing them regularly for a long time will help them stick in your brain and become part of your thinking.

* * *

PHRASE BY PHRASE

This is probably the most basic, simple way to memorize. Simply read the first phrase of the verse or passage until you can say it without looking. Then do the same with the next phrase. Then put the two phrases together and repeat them until you can say them together without looking. Then take the next phrase and continue in the same way until the whole verse or passage is memorized.

READING AND REPEATING

This is similar to the previous suggestion. Many people like to read an entire verse ten times, then be able to recite it without looking ten times, before considering it memorized. Andrew Davis takes this approach in his *Approach to Extended Memorization* (more on this resource below).

KEEP IT IN FRONT OF YOU

For visual learners, looking at the verse often can help cement it in your mind. Try writing it on a sticky note or a whiteboard you look at often. You could also make or download a verse wallpaper for your phone's lock screen—that way you'll be looking at Scripture every time you check your phone!

LISTEN UP

For auditory learners, listening to Scripture can be invaluable. YouVersion, Blue Letter Bible, Bible Gateway, The Verses Project, and many other websites and apps offer options for listening to the word. You can also download an audio Bible, or even record yourself reading the verse you want to memorize. Listening at a faster speed is often helpful too.

DRAW IT OUT

For visual learners, drawing out a passage on paper or screen can help stick the verse in your mind. You don't even need art skills! Shapes and bright colors are all that's necessary. The crazier and more creative, the better!

VANISHING WORDS

Try writing out the verse on a whiteboard or just a piece of paper. Read it to yourself, then erase or cover up one or two words and read it again. Keep removing words until they're all gone and you can recite the passage from memory.

THE LOCI METHOD

The loci method is a more complicated memorization tool that's most helpful with longer passages, especially non-narrative books such as Psalms and Proverbs. A simplified version would work as follows: Pick a place you're familiar with. It could be your bedroom, church, classroom, or a friend's house. Chart an imaginary path through that place. Then think up an image for each phrase of the verse—the more creative, the better. Mentally place these images at points along the path you've chosen. If they can interact with each other or with objects on the path, they'll be even more memorable. When you mentally walk along that path, you'll see the images in your head and remember which phrase of the verse comes next. If you want to learn more about this method, see https://artofmemory.com/wiki/How_to_Build_a_Memory_Palace.

APPS AND ONLINE RESOURCES

An Approach to Extended Memorization of Scripture by Andrew Davis is a booklet available for free as a PDF. It is an excellent method for memorizing entire books of the Bible. Available at https://www.fbcdurham.org/resources/scripture-memory/.

BibleMemory.com—I use BibleMemory mostly for review, but it also includes memorization tools. Available at https://bible memory.com/ and in app stores for Android and iOS.

The Verses Project—Professionally recorded songs and beautiful artwork for dozens of verses and passages. The verses are in the English Standard Version. Available at http://theverses project.com/.

GLOSSARY OF ABBREVIATIONS AND KEY TERMS

apocalyptic: Literature that relates prophecies and information about the end times, usually with extravagant imagery and symbolism. The book of Revelation is apocalyptic.

apostolic: A term that describes the books of the New Testament written by the apostles and others associated with Jesus and inspired by the Holy Spirit.

application: The process of applying the truth of a passage to yourself and letting it change you (the third pillar of the inductive study method).

cf.: Abbreviation of the Latin word *confer*, meaning "compare."

canon: The collection of books recognized as the inspired word of God (cf. Old Testament, New Testament, Hebrew Scriptures).

context: Other material that "goes with" the text you're studying and helps you interpret it, including surrounding text (biblical context) as well as information about the historical setting and culture in which it was written (historical and cultural context).

cross-reference: Another portion of Scripture that relates to the passage you're studying and can expand your understanding of it.

Epistles: Those books of the New Testament that were originally letters from the apostles and other church fathers to churches or individuals.

ESV: English Standard Version (a Bible translation).

general revelation: What God has made known about himself through his creation.

Gospels: Those books of the New Testament that tell of Jesus's ministry on earth.

Hebrew Scriptures: The collection of writings that make up the Christian Old Testament, acknowledged by the Jewish people as the word of God. These would have been the "Bible" of Jesus and the apostles.

inductive study: The method of Bible study where we come first to God's word to discover him, making the Bible the primary authority and letting it interpret itself.

interpretation: The process of discovering what a passage means (the second pillar of the inductive study method).

justification: The legal action by which God declares that Jesus Christ has taken the punishment we deserved for our sin and has counted his perfect righteousness as ours, thus allowing us to have free and open fellowship with him.

key word: A word that is central to the meaning of a passage.

KJV: King James Version (a Bible translation).

lexicon: A Greek or Hebrew word study tool that lists words alphabetically according to the Greek or Hebrew alphabet and gives detailed definitions for the different instances where they're used.

meditation: The biblical discipline of dwelling on a verse or truth and letting it move you to prayer, praise, and confession.

metanarrative: A larger narrative that encompasses many smaller stories.

NASB: New American Standard Bible (a Bible translation).

New Testament: The collection of books of the Bible written after Christ's first coming and by his authority, concerned mainly with his earthly ministry and with the church (cf. Apostolic).

observation: The process of discovering what a passage says (the first pillar of the inductive study method).

observation questions: The six questions to ask of every text you study: Who? What? When? Where? Why? How?

Old Testament: The collection of books of the Bible written before Christ's first coming, concerned mainly with the nation of Israel and looking forward to Christ (cf. Hebrew Scriptures).

paraphrase: Putting a passage into your own words. This is a helpful tool for observation and interpretation.

protagonist: The main character of a story; the one around whom the story revolves.

revealed will: God's will for our lives, as revealed through his commandments in Scripture.

sanctify/sanctification: The process of becoming more like Christ after being saved.

special revelation: God's direct communication to us through the Scriptures.

TSK: *Treasury of Scripture Knowledge* (cf. Appendix A)

NOTES

Chapter 1: You Are Not Too Young

1. J. I. Packer, *Knowing God* (Downers Grove, IL: InterVarsity Press, 1973), 29.

2. Jen Wilkin, "What Student Ministry Really Needs? Homework." *Christianity Today*, November 27, 2017, http://www.christianitytoday.com/ct /2017/december/wilkin-student-ministry-really-needs-bible-homework .html.

Chapter 2: How God Reveals Himself

1. John Calvin, *Institutes of the Christian Religion*, trans. Henry Beveridge (Grand Rapids, MI: Eerdmans, 1962), 51.

2. Calvin, *Institutes*, 62.

3. Calvin, *Institutes*, 62.

4. Francis Schaeffer, *He Is There and He Is Not Silent* in *The Complete Works of Francis Schaeffer: A Christian Worldview*, 3rd ed., 5 vols. (Wheaton, IL: Crossway, 1982), 1:276.

5. Schaeffer, *He Is There and He Is Not Silent*, 1:275.

6. Calvin, *Institutes*, 46.

7. John Piper, *A Peculiar Glory: How the Christian Scriptures Reveal Their Complete Truthfulness* (Wheaton, IL: Crossway, 2016), 75.

8. Piper, *Peculiar Glory*, 56.

9. Piper, *Peculiar Glory*, 64.

10. Paul D. Wegner, *The Journey from Texts to Translations* (Grand Rapids, MI: Baker, 1999), 101.

11. Calvin, *Institutes*, 69.

12. *The Westminster Catechism* quoted in Piper, *Peculiar Glory*, 13.

13. Piper, *Peculiar Glory*, 211.

Notes

Chapter 3: The Big Story

1. I am greatly indebted to Dr. Charles Bayliss for most of the ideas in this chapter. His teaching, both in person and in the *Biblical Story* videos at http://thebiblicalstory.org/, is the origin of much of my thinking on this subject.
2. John Piper, *Fifty Reasons Why Jesus Came to Die* (Wheaton, IL: Crossway, 2006), 21.
3. J. I. Packer, *Knowing God* (Downers Grove, IL: InterVarsity Press, 1973), 50.

Chapter 4: God's Will for My Life

1. John Piper, "What Is the Will of God and How Do We Know It?" (sermon, August 22, 2004) Desiring God, https://www.desiringgod.org/messages-what-is-the-will-of-god-and-how-do-we-know-it.
2. Timothy Keller, "God's Law" (sermon, May 27, 2000), Gospel in Life, https://gospelinlife.com/downloads\god-s-law-5533/.
3. John Piper, "What Is the Origin of Desiring God's Slogan?" (interview with Tony Reinke, September 20, 2017) Desiring God, https://www.desiringgod.org/interviews/whats-the-origin-of-desiring-gods-slogan.
4. John Piper, "Why the Law Was Given" (sermon, November 15, 1981), Desiring God, https://www.desiringgod.org/messages/why-the-law-was-given.

Chapter 5: How to Obey God's Will

1. Timothy Keller, "How to Change" (sermon, April 19, 1998), Gospel in Life, https://gospelinlife.com/downloads\how-to-change-5960/.

Chapter 6: Part of Your Life

1. Jen Wilkin, *Women of the Word: How to Study the Bible with Both Our Hearts and Our Minds* (Wheaton, IL: Crossway, 2014), 83.
2. David Mathis, *Habits of Grace: Enjoying Jesus through the Spiritual Disciplines* (Wheaton, IL: Crossway, 2016), 43.
3. Wilkin, *Women of the Word*, 123.
4. Mathis, *Habits of Grace*, 146.
5. C. S. Lewis, *The Four Loves*, in *The Beloved Works of C. S. Lewis* (New York: Inspirational Press, 1984), 255.

Chapter 7: Getting Started with Bible Study

1. Jen Wilkin, *Women of the Word: How to Study the Bible with Both Our Hearts and Our Minds* (Wheaton, IL: Crossway, 2014), 103. Much of this section was inspired by Jen Wilkin's more thorough chapter "Study with Prayer" in *Women of the Word*.
2. Text for this illustration was taken from the ESV® Bible (The Holy Bible, English Standard Version®), copyright © 2001 by Crossway, a

publishing ministry of Good News Publishers. Used by permission. All rights reserved.

3. Wilkin, *Women of the Word*, 75.

Chapter 10: Interpretation

1. Text for this sample page is from the ESV® Bible (The Holy Bible, English Standard Version®), copyright © 2001 by Crossway, a publishing ministry of Good News Publishers. Used by permission. All rights reserved.

2. Text for this illustration comes from James Strong, *Strong's Exhaustive Concordance of the Bible* (Peabody, MA: Hendrickson, 2009).

Chapter 11: Application

1. J. I. Packer, *Knowing God* (Downers Grove, IL: InterVarsity Press, 1973), 17.

2. John Piper, "The Ultimate Goal of Reading the Bible" (sermon, Skamania Lodge, Stevenson, Washington, September 23, 2016), Desiring God, https://www.desiringgod.org/messages/the-ultimate-goal-of-reading-the-bible.

3. David Mathis, *Habits of Grace: Enjoying Jesus through the Spiritual Disciplines* (Wheaton, IL: Crossway, 2016), 64–65.

4. Jaquelle Crowe, *This Changes Everything: How the Gospel Transforms the Teen Years* (Wheaton, IL: Crossway, 2017).

5. Packer, *Knowing God*, 18.

6. Packer, *Knowing God*, 18–19.

7. Mathis, *Habits of Grace*, 72.

Epilogue

1. "Shelby Kennedy: The Story behind National Bible Bee," National Bible Bee (website), https://biblebee.org/about/beginnings/.

GENERAL INDEX

SCRIPTURE INDEX

Thoughts

Thoughts

Thoughts

Thoughts

Thoughts

Thoughts

Thoughts

Thoughts

Thoughts

Thoughts

Thoughts